WHEN THE
VISION
— HAS —
VANISHED

WHEN THE VISION HAS VANISHED

The Story of a Pastor and the Loss of a Church

Robert C. Girard

Edited by Audrey I. Girard

Ministry Resources Library

Zondervan Publishing House • Grand Rapids, MI

WHEN THE VISION HAS VANISHED

Ministry Resources Library is an imprint of Zondervan Publishing House, 1415
Lake Drive S.E., Grand Rapids, Michigan, 49506

Library of Congress Cataloging-in-Publication Data

Girard , Robert C.
  When the vision has vanished : the story of a pastor and the loss of a
church / Robert C. Girard ; edited by Audrey I. Girard.
        p.   cm.
  Includes bibliographical references.
  ISBN 0-310-39221-7
  1. Pastoral theology. 2. Girard, Robert C. 3. Our Heritage Church (Scotts-
dale, Ariz.) 4. Failure (Christian theology) 5. Success—Religious aspects—
Christianity. I. Girard, Audrey I. II. Title.
BV4011.G495   1989   89-37644
253—dc20   CIP

Editor: Susan Lutz
Designer: James E. Ruark

Printed in the United States of America

89 90 91 92 93 94 / PP / 10 9 8 7 6 5 4 3 2 1

*To the people who meet as the church
at Montezuma Chapel,
who took a wounded brother
into their arms
and helped him heal.*

Contents

Contents

Acknowledgments

The encouragement of these people has been vital to the completion of this book: Larry Richards, who carried the first sketchy outline to Michael Smith of Zondervan; Michael Smith, whose interest and personal affirmation of the value of what I have to say got me going; Estelle Cresswell, who provided word-processing equipment, which makes writing such a "breeze"; Rod Wilke, Shirley Tyler, and Kitt Nelson, who read the unedited manuscript and by wise advice helped shape the final draft; the survivors and observers of Our Heritage Church, who helped me evaluate what happened there; my wife and closest co-worker, Audrey Girard, whose love, support, spiritual discernment, and editorial skills are indispensable to my writing and my life.

Thanks!

Acknowledgments

Popular Models for Dealing With Failure

Success is never final.
Failure is never fatal.
It's courage that counts.

—Winston Churchill

THE RICHARD NIXON MODEL

Cover it up.

THE DON LARSEN MODEL

Think only of your success. Replay the films of your World Series no-hitter.

THE JIM AND TAMMY BAKKER MODEL

Refuse to take the blame. Shed lots of crocodile tears. Threaten to sue.

THE CHUCK COLSON MODEL

Accept the verdict. Serve your time. Start a new ministry to help others who have failed as you have.

THE ROBERT SCHULLER MODEL

Every failure is inherently pregnant with some positive possibility. Turn your failures into an investment that can increase your productivity! Have you failed? Many people will want to know why. Capitalize on their curiosity! Become a consultant!

THE ABRAHAM AND SARAH MODEL

Live with your mistake and try again.

THE JACOB MODEL

Face up to your failure with an attitude of humility and servanthood. Wrestle with God until he blesses you. Send your enemy a gift. Be ready to take your lumps.

THE JOSEPH MODEL

Don't compromise with sin. Don't expect justice. Do what you can where you are—even in jail. And get out as soon as you can.

THE MOSES MODEL

Get away to the backside of the desert until *God* says, "Go back and face 'em again."

THE KING DAVID MODEL

Face up to your failure. Repent of your sin. Take your punishment. Receive forgiveness. Get up and go on.

THE JUDAS ISCARIOT MODEL

Hang yourself. Be replaced. Set your failure in concrete.

THE SIMON PETER MODEL

Shed a lot of bitter tears. Go fishing for a while. Feed God's sheep.

THE JESUS MODEL

Rise again . . . and prove them wrong.

Chapter 1

Face to Face With Failure

> We can only appreciate the miracle of a sunrise if we have waited in the darkness. —*Wes Yamaka*[1]

"MY LIFE IS OVER!"

I glared at my reflection in the bathroom mirror through reddened eyes and clutched the sides of the sink in a white-knuckle grip. I hated the face in the mirror. Inner pain spat into words every forbidden epithet, hurling them into the face in the glass.

At age forty-seven it seemed that every important aspect of my life was a scene of irreparable failure. My wife was weeping in another room, our relationship torturously strained by the bitterness that boiled out of my witch's cauldron of anger and guilt. My teenage son lay on his bed brooding over his dad's irrational behavior after slamming the bedroom door in justified disgust. Muffled sobs from my youngest daughter's room completed the circle of family turmoil.

The church (my "life's work") into which I had poured my blood, sweat, and tears for fourteen years was on the verge of disintegration. My friends felt I had forsaken them. I had. My ecclesiastical peers had washed their hands of me. My reputation was destroyed. I was a laughingstock among those whose respect I needed. And I was in the throes of emotional breakdown.

Hopelessness was never so rampant, faith never so useless.

As I stood there facing myself in the glass, I despised the spiritual cripple that these devastations had left behind. Actually he was no stranger. His spiritual impotence had been apparent for many years. But in the backwash of failure, his deformity was impossible to hide.

There was no future. Nothing to live for. The thought of going on living another twenty years was nearly unthinkable. I wished for death. I did more than wish. As I sank into self-pity, in my mind *I planned my death!* The thought gave me a sick comfort in the midst of my personal hell.

At that moment I was sure God hated me as much as I thought everyone else did, and as much as I hated myself.

Some might try to tell me that as a Christian I should not have felt, thought, and acted that way. Yet as a Christian I did, and nobody understood that I "shouldn't have" more than I. It just added to the list of failures that were convincing me—"My life is over!"

Success? I have touched it fleetingly, as it flitted off to make its home with someone else.

Failure? It and I have lived together as one. I know failure . . . at least from the human perspective.

My story is a record of the failure of a man and the faithfulness of God, of starting over, and of life after fiasco. It has been a long and difficult process of refocusing and regaining lost perspective. It has cost the people near me dearly. And it is far from over. But I am not discouraged. I'm no longer on the bottom. I'm alive. I survived my death wishes and my failures by the grace of God! God sees our crises quite differently from the way we do. According to the perspective of the Bible, God always meets failure with grace.

To set the scene for God's joyful perspective, I should begin by telling you the story of my descent into grief.

THE CHURCH WITH A NEW FACE

In the late 1960s I was the founding pastor of an unusual church. It started out as an immediate success, growing along the lines of many good, traditional, evangelical churches. But early on, something very exciting began to happen that changed the church completely. It catapulted me and the church into an unexpected place of influence. We became fed up with the evangelical status quo and full to the brim with a passion to return to a New Testament style and quality of church life.

Our Heritage Church in Scottsdale, Arizona (lovingly dubbed "O.H."), brought together an incongruous mix of pioneers, visionaries, church dropouts, ecclesiastical and emotional misfits, spiritual cripples, wounded healers, sightseers, and saints. Some of us were angry young dreamers on an exciting adventure. A vision of the church as it could be drove us on. We did not know where it would take us, but we were sure that the Spirit of God was leading the march and that a wonderful experience of the body of Christ was within our reach . . . if we were willing to die for it.

Pain and struggle and rejection were borne with courage and joy. We stood alone against the world, our religious peers, and accepted ecclesiastical structures. Friends and fellow members forsook us, but we clung to each other. And hope never waned.

We loved each other. Fought and argued with each other. Yelled at each other. And hammered out consensus on some extremely difficult doctrinal issues. But we continued to love one another in the face of it.

Even today, most of those who were part of this intense body remember one thing more than any other—*the love.*

It was certainly not heaven. Not even the Millennium. We knew full well that we were in the trenches of a hand-to-hand war. Sometimes we joked about it, sometimes took pride in it, sometimes felt depressed about it. And we were such a bunch of misfits! Deeply needy, one and all, leaders as well as followers.

Leading the charge was a cadre of men we called "the pastoral team" (or elders). To me, it was liberating to share shepherding responsibilities in consensus with such a team. We were all weak men in many ways, a fact we readily admitted to one another and the church. Leading from weakness, we were able to emancipate some people from pretense and hypocrisy. People who were seeking a strong man to admire and in whom they could find answers were sometimes frustrated.

Eventually our vision exceeded our ability to live out what we saw. We did not understand how weak we really were. This good church simply disappeared from the landscape, its new wine oozing out of unhealed cracks and finding its way into other skins.

THE FACE OF SUCCESS

In the early years of Our Heritage Church, I wrote a book that became a Christian best-seller with more than 100,000 copies in print.[2] I found myself on the leading edge of a spontaneous movement that looked as if it might profoundly affect the direction of the evangelical church world. I preached and lectured across the country in conferences, seminars, colleges, and seminaries. My book was required reading in seminary courses.

The church I founded, though small, was widely known, lively, and influential. Scores of people were introduced to Christ through its ministry. Together we were engaged in some significant pioneering in church life, forms, and leadership. A true community was developing, a spiritual family, in which relationships with and love for one another flourished.

Phone calls and letters came from around the world.

Readers called to ask about the concepts in the book and about problems in their churches.

Audrey and I were invited on a preaching-teaching tour of the major cities of Australia, where my book had sold more per capita than anywhere else in the world. It was translated into German and distributed in Europe. I even received mail from behind the Iron Curtain. A mission organization wrote, indicating that they were considering a Japanese translation.

Christianity Today republished my book in the same volume with books by Billy Graham and Francis Schaeffer.[3] (Pretty rich company, I thought.)

I was asked to write a regular column in a national evangelical magazine.

And my second book was published.[4]

I found myself "sharing the platform" and, sometimes, quality personal time with such people as David and Karen Mains, Ray Stedman, Larry Richards, Lloyd Ogilvie, and David Hubbard.[5]

Meanwhile, back at the church, danger lurked in ambush. The coming firestorm would leave me with serious questions about the value of everything I had ever done.

My life, my feelings about myself, my sense of value had been interwoven with the people and the destiny of that church. A man should see himself in God, with intrinsic personal value apart from the work in which he is engaged. But I could never do that. During my years at O.H., people would become frustrated with the church and leave, saying, "But, Bob, we still love you." Inside, I would find such a statement incomprehensible. If you loved me, you would not be separating yourself from my ministry, my work, and my church.

In the same way, I had found it impossible to see myself as separate from the failures and weaknesses of the church. They were *my* failures, *my* weaknesses. And the church's death? That would be the death of *me!*

In a crucial decision near the end of the church's life (which I'll detail later), the elders led the congregation out of its buildings and into informal house-church groups. Such house churches are flourishing and multiplying in other parts of the world. In this new form, O.H. could have continued to influence the evangelical movement with fresh, exciting exploits in discipling, evangelism, and *koinonia*.

But that is not what happened.

Notes

1. Quoted by Mary Carter Smith, "Eugene," *Faith at Work* (September-October 1988): 5.
2. *Brethren, Hang Loose* (Grand Rapids: Zondervan, 1972).
3. *Books for Believers*, vol. 1 (New York: Iverson-Norman Associates, 1972). This is a Christianity Today Trilogy, including Billy Graham's *Jesus Generation*, Francis A. Schaeffer's *True Spirituality*, and Robert C. Girard's *Brethren, Hang Loose*.
4. *Brethren, Hang Together* (Grand Rapids: Zondervan, 1979).
5. Dynamic Church Ministries (DCM), a group of evangelicals committed to aiding the cause of church renewal, held seminars in many U.S. and some foreign cities during the 1970s and engaged in experimental projects such as Step 2 curriculum, under the leadership of Lawrence O. Richards, David Mains, and Clyde Hoeldtke.

Chapter 2

When All the Walls Came Tumbling Down

O death, where is your sting?
O grave, your victory?
You came to make an end,
Beginning comes to me.
You chose to make it dark,
I find a great new Light.
You're bound to kill my flesh,
Releasing me to life!

— *Audrey Girard*

O.H. WAS A *GOOD* CHURCH!

At times it was crazy, scary, frustrating, and wrong-headed, but you could do things in that church you couldn't do anywhere else. You could do something crazy just to see if it would fly! Like turning the pews around so people could look into each other's faces when they sang and shared. Like interrupting the whole service just to listen to somebody's

21

problem and to gather around him and pray. Like asking for questions and even debate after the Sunday morning sermon. Like letting needy people live in the church building.

There was freedom. Joy and laughter sometimes—real delight in each other. Sharing that sometimes dared to get personal and real.

People listened to each other in that church. If a troubled college football player needed an hour to try to say what he needed to say, even if it made us nervous, most would give him the room he needed. Nobody cared if the service ran half a day. (Well, that's an overstatement. The length of some of the services drove some of us crazy. But we were more committed to giving people time and room than to ending the meetings at a specified time.)

We could get away with not having fancy programming. Just being together was sometimes enough. People came first, not the institution or the program. Our meetings were often sloppy and disjointed, but they were personal and dealt with the realities of our lives. Neatness, after all, is not all that counts in the family of God.

I'm not suggesting that everyone bought into all of this. Many could not and did not. Some suffered with it for a while, then left. But I don't know very many places where such liberties would even be permitted in the first place.

Caring happened. We went a long, long way in tolerating sinners—too far, sometimes. But people with monumental spiritual problems often felt accepted and loved, and some got help.

Personal growth and needed change took place in our lives. I know they did in mine. A common theme running through the testimonies of people who were with us for any length of time is, "We will never be the same. We grew. We learned to love." I asked some of them to evaluate the ministry of Our Heritage Church. Here's a sampling:

"We learned to love one another. Prayer was our greatest privilege and responsibility. We were and still are a family of God being bonded together by Jesus. . . . We came to learn and were taught the Word of God. We learned to open our hearts to Jesus and each other. We shared each other's burdens by prayer, helping, sharing, and fellowship. We experienced great joy by singing and just being together."—*Mary Lazear*

"It was a courageous, Scripture-responsive break with tradition that produced some excellent responses: freedom, expression of love, emphasis on personal growth. It provided the environment for change and growth. . . . The elders had something very special in the way our relationships developed into deeper and more intense ones."—*Rod Wilke*

"The ministry to me was a 'setting free' ministry. For the first time in my life I met Christians who weren't perfect and weren't ashamed to say so. The people at O.H. fought, struggled, questioned, and really tried to be honest about their relationships with God and other people. It was exactly what I needed."—*Rick Jacobs*

"You were successful in discipling a rebellious and undisciplined young man and giving him a desire to know God and to make him known. You poured your life into him for seven years and he will never forget your love and understanding."— *Ron Rogers, youth director*

"O.H. was a visible example of men and women of God who were attempting to break out of empty routines and meaningless activities to find the New Testament promise of life in Jesus Christ. O.H. challenged us to have courage in exploring this *life* as a family. It acted on the discoveries people were making. It opened the door for many of us to take new steps. We found camaraderie so that we didn't have to take these new steps alone."—*Norm Wakefield, branch church pastor*

"It was a very exciting church with a vibrancy of spiritual growth. Members were ministering to each other. Whenever I met one of them, they seemed anxious to share what the Lord was doing in their lives. . . . There seemed to be a sense of ownership; everyone seemed to feel like an integral part of the body, each a living member of the whole."—*Erich Hoeffer, neighboring pastor*

Sure, there were things *wrong* with O.H., and plenty of

things that *went* wrong. I often felt ripped apart, as a secret, inner war raged between the old patterns I'd been raised with and the strange new things that were happening before my eyes. When someone had had enough and left the church, I felt as if part of my heart had been taken with them. Tears were a large part of Our Heritage, an ongoing contrast with the joy.

Our leaders were wrong about a lot of things. We didn't really understand how to shepherd, guide, and help in such a strange, new style of church life. But we didn't try to arbitrarily control everybody and everything either.

We developed subtle prejudices against planning, professionalism, and excellence. We were suspicious of organization, and some less visible people were missed in our ministry. We doted on the excitement of spontaneity and tended to see it as the only real thing. Some people with less spontaneous gifts (including some of our best musicians) felt unwanted and out of place.

But even with such blind spots, there was more freedom and affirmation for the average Christian than I have seen anywhere else in the church. We felt priorities were being brought into line with biblical imperatives. Committed workers (about thirty) were called by the Lord and sent by the church into various Christian ministries. Leaders had freedom to experiment, trying to find more edifying and effective ways of doing and being the church. As a people we were getting loose to dare to be ourselves, in front of God and everybody!

Yet now it's gone. How could such a terrible thing happen to such a promising young church?

The failure of Our Heritage Church cannot simply be attributed to the elders' decision to lead the congregation out of its buildings and into informal house-church groups. In other parts of the world, house churches like those we envisioned have succeeded. We were excited about the spiritual possibilities as we left our institutional setting and launched out on the new adventure.

But within months, the congregation had been reduced to a scattered flock. Most of the house churches had disintegrated.

Some of their people were finding their way into established, traditional churches. Some seemed lost, groping for direction. The "shepherds" went their separate ways, each struggling with his own questions and wondering what had gone wrong. No one was lost to the kingdom, but . . .

Today in Scottsdale, Arizona, there exists no monument to my work of fifteen years. The congregation that meets in the building we once occupied contains a few former "Our Heritage people," but it has no connection with the original body of believers. One branch church remains strong. Two or three tiny house groups continue in the neighborhood. But that vibrant group of pioneers who once shared life together as O.H. is gone.

A church is not supposed to disappear. Ecclesiastical brass will sometimes decide to close a church that has shrunk and can no longer pay its bills. But even a church that strays from the truth often goes on for generations! For a church to vanish without a trace indicates a failure to mount even the most elemental kind of success. *True?*

No one has struggled with these realities more than I. Later in this book, a "postmortem" will attempt to explain what went wrong, so that the seeds of our failure can, even yet, bear fruit.

CHURCH FAILURE IS A FACT OF LIFE

Church and pastoral failure are not uncommon. Lyle Schaller writes,

> At least three out of four of all Protestant congregations in North America that were established before 1965 once had a higher level of attendance at Sunday morning worship than they report today. In at least five denominations that proportion is nine out of ten. . . . This has occurred during an era when the combined attendance of all non-Catholic Christian churches in the United States has been setting new records year after year.[1]

We've all visited churches that were built to house hundreds, but whose present congregations have shrunk to a committed-but-discouraged handful of aging stalwarts, assembling in a near-empty monument to yesterday. A sadness hangs about them like a funeral drape. It's the melancholy that accompanies failure.

Most of the three-out-of-four or nine-out-of-ten churches Schaller cites did not disappear as Our Heritage did. But if success is measured in terms of statistical growth or holding our own, *most* churches are not succeeding, and their pastors and leaders may well be struggling with a nagging sense of failure—not as intense as mine, perhaps, but embarrassingly real nonetheless. The point is that when I write about failure in this book, about what I've learned from it, and how I've been able to go on living with it on my record, there's a good chance that a lot of Christians will identify with the story I'm telling.

In the Bible, God takes a very different approach from humans for evaluating the success or failure of a man or a church. Statistics have little to do with it. The congregation rattling around in the monstrous hall of yesteryear could be succeeding in God's terms. Success has nothing to do with history or physical location or size. It has to do with being rich toward God and with the extent to which Christ is being formed in us.

But my story of spiritual disaster is more than the story of a church. It is *my* story, the story of personal failure, the "death" of a churchman.

OUT OF STEP WITH MOTHER

Born, raised, ordained, and bound in commitment and relationship to an evangelical denomination, I looked to my ecclesiastical peers and leaders for friendship, support, and a sense of where I fit in God's plan. The connections were deeply emotional, like the bonding between child and mother. When my biological mother died during my youth, loyalty and bonding seemed to be transferred to my "mother church."

But I chose a different approach to ministry than most of my colleagues. To tell it as I experienced it: I *felt led* to follow a path I was convinced was more biblical. And gradually I became more and more out of step with "mother."

Our denomination was suspicious. We in O.H. felt the disdain of many who thought us naive and foolish. Nearly every change we made was opposed by someone.

Meeting with district leaders, our elders tried to explain why we had chosen the direction we were taking, trying to show from Scripture and church history where we were coming from. One official responded, "If these things are correct, why hasn't God revealed them to some *smart* person?" I had no answer. I always thought it was too bad God couldn't have found smarter people to take these risks.

When our local team of elders decided to give the church buildings and land back to the denomination and to strike out "on our own" as a string of unencumbered house churches, district and denominational leaders had had enough of our experimentation and nonconformity. We were expelled for having departed "too far from the norm." Ironic. Our tradition looked back to John Wesley, who was rejected by the Anglican Church for his radical preaching, his house churches (class meetings), and his use of lay preachers—the things that put us beyond "the norm."

While I had always admitted that such a break was possible, given the off-beat direction our local church was going, I was not ready for such monumental rejection. And it was not just the church relationship that was severed; my ministerial credentials were withdrawn too! It was as though I had let my mother down, and she had thrown me out.

We are talking here about the severing of a relationship that I had had since birth. I had never taken a breath of life outside. Even though I had been a rebellious son and caused my "mother" pain, I had always believed the relationship would go on—somehow—till death.

In a few months a neighboring state district of the same denomination restored my membership and ministerial credentials. But whenever I meet any of my denominational colleagues, I always have the feeling that I am a black sheep tolerated in the flock. I am the prodigal who never returned . . . not really. I am the poor slob who couldn't keep his act together, who failed, leaving an ugly smear on the face of the church.

From a dollars-and-cents perspective, a public relations perspective, an organization perspective, they could hardly be expected to view it any other way. For all her considerable investment in me, I left the "mother church" with nothing but problems and disgrace.

"THERAPY? WHAT KIND OF A PREACHER ARE YOU?"

I felt more than heard scornful questions from people as I surrendered myself to the painful processes of primal integration therapy. The disintegration of O.H. and the ecclesiastical rebuke had put my problems beyond me. I had already put off seeking help for so long that it was threatening my marriage. My outbursts of anger were becoming more and more destructive. I had lived with these problems (and so had my family) for a long, long time. Time enough to have tried everything the church suggested: prayer, confession, all the touted spiritual experiences, the classic spiritual disciplines. Most were helpful. The sharing-and-accepting atmosphere of our church family made confession easier. But nothing brought the healing I needed. I could put it off no longer. If the church could not heal me, then I must seek help outside the church.

The help I found was a form of primal integration therapy conducted by a Christian therapist trained in Cecil Osborne's Yokefellow program.[2] The basic approach was borrowed from secular psychology. Standard personality inventories were used. Though I had many misgivings, the Lord gave me a sense of peace that this was the right thing for me to do.

Some people understood. They carried me through the process with their prayers, encouragement, and money. Others fell strangely silent. There was that persistent (and not unjustified) suspicion by Christians against psychologists and psychiatrists and their science. Some of my friends openly argued that Christians should seek their emotional healing only in the context of the prayer meeting and the spiritual formulas and experiences that accompany the faith. But I was sure I had tried them all.

Primal therapy has led me to some answers. Yet, at low times I am quite vulnerable to the suggestion that my emotional weaknesses and the necessity of going outside the church for help, did, indeed, represent colossal spiritual defeat . . . *failure.*

BROKEN RELATIONSHIPS

My three-year firestorm of failure was marked at nearly every turn by relational breakdown.

Denominational separation brought an instant end to friendships that once had seemed warm and real. People with whom we had worked, with whom we had lived through so many struggles, and with whom we had shared so much of life now avoided us.

I did my share of forsaking friends too. As I sorted out my life during this chaotic period, I left the paid professional ministry. In therapy I began to touch feelings toward my life's work that I had never faced—feelings of distaste and the desire to be free of pastoral responsibility altogether. I discovered that in many of my relationships, even with colleagues I loved dearly, I felt trapped. Now I felt I had to be free.

So I asked the leadership team to release me, and I told them I was leaving the church altogether. Some of those who had been closest to me felt betrayed. Our relationships had become much more than institutional commitments. We had stood together against the tide. We had logged much personal time together, become open books to each other, supported and cared for each other on a very personal level, and stated our love in terms of a commitment to hang in there with each other "no matter what." They had invested in my healing process with money and personal support. They released me, but with expressions of bitter personal disappointment and frustration.

They felt I had failed them. I had.

Notes

1. Lyle E. Schaller, "Redundant Ties," *The Parish Paper* (530 N. Brainard St., Naperville, IL 60540).
2. Yokefellows, Inc., Burlingame, California.

Chapter 3

Requiem for a Dream

> Those who refuse to learn from the tragedies of the
> past are doomed to repeat them.   *—Aristotle*

WHEN I HIT BOTTOM personally and professionally, I was in
a position where everything in my life needed to be reexam-
ined. My goal was to see things from God's perspective, not my
own, which all too often was clouded with the confusion of
unhealed pain and untended sin.

My personal struggles as a man and as a pastor were
shared by only a few—most notably my family. But the
disappearance of O.H. was a loss that affected many people.
Many have had to learn, as I have, how to deal with the
bewilderment and the pain. My personal postmortem refuses to
end. I relive it in dreams and nightmares. It sets the agenda for
conversations with my wife when something reminds us of
"O.H. days." I strain to hear the voices of warning and
exhortation that might help avert a repeat performance.

EULOGY

To try to understand and learn from the mistakes of the past, I recently mailed out a questionnaire asking people who had been involved with the church to share their perceptions. A cover letter explained the query.

It has been more than eight years since Our Heritage Church in Scottsdale and the Wesleyan Church parted ways. Today there is little left in that area to visibly remind anyone that such a church as "O.H." ever existed. . . . Most of what remains lives in the hearts and memories of the people who were part of it.

The debate continues as to whether or not the entire project should be stamped "failure." Or if God was indeed doing something significant there, even though it never achieved what the world calls "success," and, in the end, all but disappeared as an institution. No one has struggled with these questions more than I.

Nevertheless, there are lessons to be learned and perhaps shared. So I'm working on a book to deal with what I think God has taught me through my own process of personal and professional failure—what I've learned about the nature of failure and success—and starting over. I want it to be an honest book, telling it like it is. I also want it to communicate the hope there is in Christ and the cross for people struggling with their own "failures."

In evaluating what happened at Our Heritage Church I am clearly not an "impartial observer." I'm not sure who is. So in an effort to give the truest picture, I'm asking several people who were involved from differing points of observation to evaluate it. Would you be willing to give me your evaluation?

I enclosed with the letter the following questionnaire:

Survey: What Happened at Our Heritage Church?
These questions are merely suggestive. If you can answer some or all of them, it would be helpful. If you find the questions too confining, write whatever you want.

> *1. How would you evaluate the ministry of Our Heritage Church?*
> *2. In what specific areas did the church succeed?*

3. *In what specific areas did it fail?*
4. *Do you tend to view the Our Heritage Church project as a success or a failure overall?*
5. *Please list what you see as the major factors which led to its success or failure.*

The letter and survey were sent to friends and detractors, officers and rank-and-file members, neighboring pastors and denominational officials. Some were merely observers. Most were intimates. We had lived the experience together. The smell of smoke still stings our nostrils.

To my surprise, only two in that varied list judged what happened at Our Heritage Church a failure. Even those with reason to be derogatory could see reasons to credit it as a success. One O.H. member did not think it was a question of success or failure:

> Success, failure, and project are words that I don't relate to at all when I think about what has happened to me along my spiritual walk. Debate also grates, because whatever happened at that time happened to individuals and I don't need or want my individual experience debated.
>
> So what was my personal experience at O.H.? It was the beginning of questioning, personal growth, pain, joy . . . all the stuff that brings life and a very personal relationship with the Holy Spirit within me. Most of Scripture has taken on new meaning and I feel very loved by God. My Christianity is no longer just a belief system, but an experience. Of course, Yokefellow, my therapy, and hundreds of hours of small group participation have been significant, but the people and spirit at O.H. were my launching pad (and some of them continue to be).
>
> I've worked with lots of Christians, pastors and wives, in therapy. In fact, that's all I've worked with. . . . As a result of all my experiences I grieve for the church. I see the people more bound than free, more guilty than forgiven, more lonely than loved, more pained than healed, more lost than saved, *ad infinitum*. It's a harsh judgment but it seems to me that there may be more of Satan's spirit than God's in all the churches I know

about. Fortunately, I don't know about most churches—so I hope, but I also doubt.

In my opinion, most of what went on at O.H. was much more scriptural and closer to God's heart than what goes on elsewhere (and is so popular). "The gate is narrow—contracted by pressure—and the way is straitened and compressed that leads to life, and few are they who find it." I don't know if it would have been different if we'd really understood that better at the time. I do know that there aren't many up for it. I recollect that many were willing to listen, some were willing to talk about it, few were willing to do it.

I thank God for my time at O.H.

—Juanita Ferguson, church secretary

Everyone who answered my letter had positive things to say. For example. . . .

"I view O.H. overall as a great success. At a significant moment in many of its members' lives it was the agency through which God's Spirit worked to shape them. Long after our world is dissolved and no single atom remains, that which was built into many of us will remain."—*Larry Richards, elder*

"Our Heritage began with a healthy view of grace and an exciting dependence on the Holy Spirit ministering in and through the individual believer. Concrete expression was thereby given to the priesthood of believers. . . . Body life was experienced in the worship services, as well as when the members met in small groups from house to house during the week. Liberty in the Spirit fostered openness, oneness and acceptance of others . . . diversity within unity. . . ."—*Jay Klagge, branch church pastor*

"O.H. succeeded by seeing the value of a person who wanted to hear and be heard and didn't know how to begin. It gave us a direction to go and a vision for the future. It was not willing to concretize a work, but rather to start it and cheer it on, like the apostles of old."—*Howard Graham, elder*

The consensus is that this church, though it died young, succeeded in some important ways. Respondents mentioned these "areas of success" (mostly in their words): (1) There was a sincere interest in leading people to Christ. . . . Many became true followers of the risen Lord; (2) a good number heard the call of God and are in various Christian ministries; (3) O.H. "mothered" three branch churches; (4) people who were involved grew spiritually; (5) it succeeded in involving a greater percentage of the local church in vital ministry, that ministry which generates life in another person; (6) the priesthood of believers flourished; (7) congregational life was characterized by words like "caring," "warmth," "real love," and "needs being met."; (8) diversity within unity was appreciated and applauded; (9) the elders developed deeper-than-usual relationships in the context of which decision making and ministry could be shared; (10) there was openness, honesty, good Bible education; (11) "I believe we did what God wanted us to do."

So what went wrong? I'm still mulling over the insights my respondents shared. I continue to listen very carefully to what each one has to say.

SURVIVORS' POSTMORTEM

Good churches don't just up and die. Not without good reason. With all she had going for her, Our Heritage carried along the dead weight of serious weaknesses that contributed to her dissolution. The following are comments of O.H. insiders. (These are mostly the respondents' own words, condensed and edited.)

A shift of focus from Christ to renewal

Somewhere in the process our focus shifted slowly, subtly, quietly, and quite devastatingly away from Jesus to renewal.—*Ron Rogers, youth director*

New forms became ends in themselves ("our distinctive form of worship"). The movement became man-centered, self-centered, and somewhat smug, instead of centered in the work of Jesus Christ and focused on his person.—*Jay Klagge*

The unrealized promise of evangelism

Evangelism failed to happen the way we said it would—spontaneously because of love for Jesus.—*Ron Rogers*

There were many conversions that did not translate into a growth in church membership. This is the real measure of any ministry.—*Larry Richards*

Words failing to translate to action

We could convince ourselves intellectually, but could not get the emotional intensity needed to make personal change possible.—*Rod Wilke*

Many were willing to listen, some were willing to talk about being a scriptural church, few were willing to do it.—*Juanita Ferguson*

Leadership unpreparedness and ineffectiveness

The church failed as an institution. Its leadership was not able to develop structures for life together which permitted the body *as an organization* to maintain itself and to multiply. Personal baggage carried by many of the leaders made O.H. an act of rebellion versus the church, rather than a calling of love.—*Larry Richards*

Multiple leadership like that tried at O.H. is a very difficult system to make work.—*Ron Rogers*

I greatly admired the men in leadership at O.H., but I don't think at the time they were "together" enough to disciple the young men in the church.—*Rick Jacobs*

We (the elders) shared a very special kind of relationship. But we failed to bring the "inner man" into the light. We continued to hide from one another. We all shared a common thread of anger, which colored our perceptions of both people and Scripture. Our hidden anger did not seriously hinder our theology and interpretation of Scripture, but it made a dramatic difference in the way we dealt with people. It shaped the words and emotions we used, and the amount of time and intensity of our follow-up. Our inability to make important personal changes kept us from becoming the models the body required.—*Rod Wilke*

O.H. did not have a sufficiently mature team of elders to lead the body through the evolving process. They were men who loved Christ, but could not provide the stability people needed. Bob's preaching spoke to the yearnings of people's hearts. He brought people along as far as he was able, then was forced to deal with his own need for inner healing. Others were not able to carry on where he left off. It was not failure. It was just what had to happen.—*Norman Wakefield, branch church pastor*

Like most businesses, leadership is the key. A man had a dream, laid out a plan, and implemented it. His experience, honesty, and ability carried the church until he got tired, lost confidence in himself, and left. This led to the end. I and others would have followed him to any other building.—*Ed Janos, church treasurer*

Caught in the waning of the Jesus Movement

Our Heritage, being part of the general revival of the late sixties and early seventies, suffered the demise of the Jesus Movement at approximately the same time and for the same general reasons.—*Jay Klagge*

The narrowness of the way

God called us to a prophetic ministry, saying things he desperately wanted to say to the church and the world. He called us to attempt to live out the principles we espoused. We tried. Sometimes we succeeded, sometimes we failed, seldom did we back off or back out. We plowed entirely new ground. I believe we did what God wanted us to do.—*Ron Rogers*

Most of what went on at O.H. was much more scriptural and closer to God's heart than what goes on elsewhere (and is

so popular). "The gate is narrow—contracted by pressure—
and the way is straitened and compressed that leads to life, and
few are they who find it."[2]—*Juanita Ferguson*

A sovereign act of God

O.H. was disassembled because God needed us to go
different places and *live* what we were taught, especially to
activate the *love* we were taught and received. We must not let
the worldly structure put us in a bind or a box. We need
freedom to obey our Lord. We are still walking in the lighted
path Jesus has prepared for us.—*Mary Lazear*

OBSERVERS' POSTMORTEM

Responses also came from people outside the O.H. family
who were in a position to observe. Here are their observations
concerning the death of the church.

Restlessness and radical change

The institution did not survive because of the constant
inner turmoil and restlessness that Bob Girard personally lived
with. This repelled strong people and drew together those with
similar restlessness, creating an imbalance. It came out in Bob's
preaching. He became the object of controversy. When people
began to leave, change and innovation increased, no doubt
leading to further inner turmoil.—*John Dunn, district superinten-
dent*

Breakdown came in part due to confusion brought on by
radical changes in services and in the physical arrangement of
the church facility. People can adjust to some change, but not if
it is constantly being readjusted week by week.—*Charles
Edwards, pastor of the church now occupying O.H.'s former buildings.*

Unwillingness to consider outside advice

If O.H. leaders and district leaders could have shared on a deeper level without being threatened, it probably would have saved some heartaches. We were all young and did not take counsel or advice readily. Why should we listen to men of long years? We "knew" what would work and set about to override some good voices. —*John Dunn*

Inadequate leadership

It appeared that in latter stages the church needed more direction. In the looseness of organization it appears some never felt the need for submitting to constituted authority. —*Jimmy Johnson, visiting preacher*

A more coordinated effort was needed to keep the house churches on course together. Without a central focal point, groups have a tendency to fragment and become competitive, even heretical. —*Charles Edwards*

There seemed to be a point at which the enemy was able to divide and conquer. The success was the pastor, enabling, inspiring, and allowing individual and small-group growth activity. Failure came when the enabling heart was removed and each group was called upon to function without some constant whole-group reviving. If the pastor had continued the position of regular enabling, it might have continued to grow. —*Erich Hoeffer, neighboring pastor*

The purpose of God

Was the disappearance of Our Heritage Church a failure, or was it a part of the purpose of God for the lives of those living stones that made that church? Were you "successful" yet blind to the working of the will of God in you? If you were running a business, your survey and inquiries would have a purpose: to analyze and evaluate why, for example, sales were down the last quarter; or why your company was so behind competitively with others; or why, with increased sales, costs are growing faster . . . and a heap of other questions pertinent to a successful company. In the church of God, I'm not sure efficiency studies or in-house audit and analysis have a purpose that could give the Master good pleasure or minister his call to his people. —*Richard Zollner, neighboring pastor*

FOUNDER'S POSTMORTEM

Like my comrades, I have struggled to find answers to the painful question, *What happened to my church?* As I have reflected on the facts and searched my heart, nine factors have emerged which, in my opinion, substantially explain the disappearance of this once-exciting fellowship.

1. *My unresolved spiritual-emotional problems.* For twenty-five years I put off seeking help for neurotic emotional patterns in my personality. Anger, paranoia, compulsiveness, and guilt increasingly disrupted personal and family peace. I did not understand what was causing these problems and was at a complete loss to know how to break the damaging patterns. Angry outbursts left my family hurting and confused and left me with serious questions about my role as a minister of the gospel. I could have and should have sought professional therapy, or at least counseling, as far back as my early twenties. But fear of tarnishing the "spiritual leader image," embarrass-ment about having to admit how "unsanctified" I was— pride—kept me from getting help and kept my family in turmoil for twenty-five years!

The series of stresses connected with our movement into house churches brought me to the edge and then pushed me over. I did not understand what was happening at the time, but I went into a period of deep mourning and depression and moved further away from reality. At a time when the local church needed leadership more than ever, I lost my desire and ability to function as a church leader. At the time when a shepherd was needed to keep the scattering flock together, I left the sheep in the care of others to tend to my own wounds, which would wait no longer for attention.

2. *Anger.* As an angry leader I tended to attract people who were angry. I failed to face up to the destructiveness of my neurotic intensity until forced to do so by the complete unraveling of my emotional stability. So instead of providing a model of how to deal constructively with anger, I provided a model of how to saturate the whole process of church leadership with it. The Holy Spirit gave me a prophetic vision, but I became as much a rebel as a prophet. Men who felt the same as I did enthusiastically joined the revolution.

The elders-pastors of Our Heritage were all angry men. We loved Jesus Christ with blazing fervor. Our personal pain gave us the urgent need for a community of love and caring. We were frustrated with the status quo and shared a vision of what the church ought to be—a vision based solidly on Scripture. And we moved toward our ideal *with a vengeance!* We shared a common impatience with those who did not wish to move as rapidly. We debated heatedly with those who disagreed. Our elders' meetings were loud and intense. We came away from them with arms around each other and often spoke our love and brotherhood openly. Inwardly, however, there was sometimes unresolved hurt that smoldered into resentment.

I was disappointed when the pastor of a sister church said their leaders did not want to meet with ours because we were too loud and expressed too much anger toward one another. I knew we were intense, but I had not worried about it, because I knew we loved each other.

Then I ran across a disturbing verse of Scripture:

The anger of man does not achieve the righteousness of God (James 1:20, NASB).

But I refused to face its seriousness. I—we—did not realize its deadly potential. I think some of us sometimes even took pride in our freedom to express it. We felt good about our rebelliousness against the religious status quo, and felt justified in our anger. It gave us meaning. But we could not see its potential to drive us apart at a time when staying together was our only hope of survival as a church.

3. *Lack of commitment to unity.* Once in their separate house churches, the shepherds of Our Heritage drifted apart rather quickly. The vision of the indispensability of unified leadership was, more than I had realized, mine. As I began to concentrate my energies on trying to keep myself together, the elders' strained relationships led to an unwillingness to go on meeting regularly to talk, affirm one another, plan, and pray. Criticism and indifference began to win out over mutual esteem. The model of unity previously visible in the fellowship of the elders faded away. Issues and personality differences became more important than fellowship. Self-interest smothered body-interest. Anger took its terrible toll, not with a lot of yelling and name-calling—nothing as palpable as that—but first with a quiet erosion of desire that evolved into a distaste for getting together. Neither the house churches nor the larger congregation could survive without pastoral consensus.

At the time of our exodus from the institutional to the house-church form,[1] one of our young leaders made an observation that turned out to be prophetic: "Our relationships with each other have got to be right, or this thing will fall apart!" It is an insight that haunts me.

Less than a year after that statement was made, I entered this in my personal journal:

It was a very painful morning. Christopher unloaded on me all his negative feelings about Steve.[2] I found myself first listening, then defending, then feeling overwhelmed by the pain of the load being dumped on me. At this point I became angry and defensive as I identified many of Steve's sins as my own. Then I fell to quietly listening, trying to hear, as Christopher pressed his points and his own unmet needs—needs he felt good pastoral models could supply for him. As the conversation continued, I sat there, hurting deeply, resenting the painful load.

I left the session to cry about it. And while I was crying and praying, Acts 15:36–41, the passage Christopher and I had been studying together when his Vesuvius erupted, came back to me like an open escape hatch.

It's the place where Paul and Barnabas have such a sharp disagreement over whether Mark should accompany them on their new mission that they split and go in opposite directions: Barnabas with John Mark to Cyprus, and Paul, with Silas (a new partner), to Asia Minor.

God continues to use them both. He may even have wanted the division to come. But the relational failure of the men obscures the sense of God's mind.

Paul and Barnabas never work together again. Paul later asked for Mark, speaking of him in very positive terms, in 1 Timothy 4. But the two pioneers and friends were never close again. It's a heartbreaking story.

I began to wonder if a final split must not be inevitable—perhaps even best, under the circumstances, for Steve and Christopher and the house churches they shepherd. Is it possible that since the division between these two men that I love so dearly has failed to yield to time or my encouragement for them to seek out each other, or my defense of Steve to Christopher and my defense of Christopher to Steve, that for the peace of the church, the growth of God's work, the freedom of the men, and the unity of the body (in the long run), that such a split should be permitted?

Their rift kills me! Tears me apart. I feel so responsible. So helpless. So hopeless. Neither man will seek the other, value the other, trust the other. And their reasons are so petty. But they each have a blind spot which, under the present pressure, resists all attempts at healing. The spirit of division hangs over our work like a killer smog! Choking, blinding, stifling. Not all that overt, but definitely hindering the process we need to be pursuing. . . .

4. *Spiritual smugness and "a new legalism."* Renewal did not stop with the first seeds of pride. The holy revolution continued, even as self-righteousness tried to devour it. But somewhere we started to lose freedom and joy and began to build new boxes into which to press one another.

For instance, in our singing we tried to maintain a balance between new Scripture songs and choruses and the solid old hymns. But resistance to the old hymns grew. Some of us began to believe that only the freer, less theological music expressed a renewed faith. (Thankfully, the pendulum had begun to swing back and an appreciation for sound, thoughtful, traditional music eventually returned.)

The guitar or no accompaniment at all came to be viewed by some as more spontaneous, more real, more "spiritual," and therefore preferable to piano or organ accompaniment. The larger instruments seemed more formal, more "traditional," more disciplined. It was a totally unbiblical assumption—consider Psalm 150, for instance, where God is praised in his sanctuary with an orchestra of at least seven kinds of instruments. Gifted musicians who felt that their gifts were no longer valued lost heart. It may have felt like renewal to some, but seeds of disunity grew in a thoughtless context of mere prejudice and spiritual ignorance.

Planning, organization, and discipline became suspect. This suspicion began as an honest reaction to the meaningless liturgies and Spiritless structures and programs prevalent in much of evangelical orthodoxy. Sincere Christians wanted the church to be a work of the Holy Spirit, not a work of the flesh and its devisings. But as the pendulum of reaction swung away from dependence on human effort toward waiting for the work of the Spirit, its arc carried us past a point where I, for one, sometimes found myself afraid to lead, uncertain of my gifts, suspicious of my structured approach to preaching, hesitant to organize or to give clear direction. I came to feel that something more spontaneous than my manuscript sermons would be closer to what God and my spiritual peers wanted and needed. I doubted my own giftedness. To lead forthrightly was tantamount to trying to take over the work of the Holy Spirit. I think there is ground for great care in these areas, lest we do exactly that, but our dread of leadership and hesitancy to lead may have left the church inadequately cared for.

We wanted to be done with legalism. We were determined

to live in grace. "The letter [of the law] kills, but the Spirit gives life" (2 Cor. 3:6). We had all died in the past from legalistic approaches to discipleship and Christian work.

We really wanted to be a holy people, but came to doubt the value of spiritual discipline. We tended to confuse responsibility and duty with bondage. In a sincere attempt to avoid the old legalism, we redefined some concepts in Scripture to remove any hint of harshness or heavy expectation on God's part. For instance, we recoiled from the concept of God as a Father *punishing* his children (i.e., Heb. 12). We really wanted to be a scriptural church. But a new "reverse legalism" sometimes made us *afraid to do what was right*. A new set of unwritten "rules for freedom" (the last thing we'd ever admit to each other) had hung itself around our necks and proceeded to corrupt our newfound liberty with uncertainty and fear.

In certain aspects of our quest for renewal, deadly rigidity and narrowness set in. Some of us, for example, found significant spiritual help and progress toward wholeness in a process involving personality testing, prayer therapy groups, and primal therapy. We began to talk and act as though "walking in the light" and "deep repentance" that leads to spiritual growth and change could only really happen this way. We rightly thanked God for important spiritual insights gained. But we found great difficulty in any discussion that tried to scrutinize these structures for weaknesses or suggested that other approaches might be just as or more biblical. Some of us put all our eggs in this basket, to the neglect of other effective and necessary means of evangelism and edification.

Again, this is not what we had set out to do. We really did want to be broad and free and open to any kind of ministry that is consistent with Scripture and energized by the Holy Spirit. But in our zeal for a new wineskin that had helped some of us personally, we became narrow and shortsighted. It became part of the *new legalism* when others who were not as sold on the psychological method felt less than fully accepted.

Our way of "doing church" became to our minds almost the only right way. Other groups, other churches, other

Christians were doing it wrong. No one else was as right as we were. No one else was as transparent, as unencumbered, as emancipated, as close to the New Testament ideal and priorities as we. We were "a renewal church." The suggestion that something real might be happening elsewhere was viewed with a jaundiced eye. Those who left for another church were viewed as "less spiritual" or "less committed to Christ." (Some might have been; but I'm not so sure as I once was.) Significantly, this problem increased as our numbers fell off and we were forced to deal with the impending sense of failure.

5. *Lack of pastoral giftedness and preparedness.* Besides my wife and kids, no group of people on the face of the earth is more precious to me than that group of Christian men who had been chosen by the congregation to serve as elders, "the pastoral team." For six years we had struggled with what it means to be shepherds of the flock of God. We had overcome many of the stereotypical definitions of lay eldership. More than any group of local leaders in any of our previous church experiences, we shared the pastoral responsibility together. We made decisions by consensus. We led from a context of fellowship with each other. Unanimously we decided that God was leading us to leave our buildings and become a collection of house churches. We were sure that this was his will for us. And we were excited about the adventure ahead.

I thought we were ready. But we were not.

As for me, I was on the verge of an emotional breakdown. And I was the one with the most experience in pastoral work. My days of usefulness as a shepherd were numbered. I was not facing up to it. The church was not prepared for my exit.

As for the others, each possessed helpful and pleasing gifts. They loved Christ and one another. Their circles of influence were growing. They were developing as teachers, counselors, and exhorters. The "edification factor" of each man's ministry was improving and doing the church good. But their lack of readiness to assume full pastoral responsibility in the house churches soon became apparent. Even in teams of two or three, something was missing. We could not see this ahead of time. Or was it that we did not *want* to see?

I am now in another pastoral situation, an older church with traditional roots. (I'll tell about it later.) We are going through a process of change with many similarities to the O.H. experience. A team of elders has been chosen to pastor the church together. Two or three years ago a man thought I was moving too slowly in releasing the ministry to others. I said I did not think that anyone else in the church was ready yet to be a pastor.

"What are you looking for?" he said. "How will a person know when he's ready?"

"When he cares about the church and the people of the church as much as I do," I said. "When he is as committed to this work as I am. When he hurts as much as I do when someone else is hurting. When he cares about the unity of the church and the health of the church and whether or not the church is fulfilling its scriptural calling. When he is ready to accept the responsibility that goes along with the job. When he is ready to work as hard at his ministry as I do. And when he can't see himself doing anything else. Then he's ready to be a pastor of this church."

I am convinced that another factor is also necessary: if a person is a spiritual leader, he or she will have a *following*. It takes time for this to develop, and if the would-be shepherd is truly gifted, it will. In the O.H. disaster, we sent men out without knowing for certain that anyone would follow them.

Even in the face of these mistakes, it might have worked had there been continuing oversight in pastoring the pastors, or had the pastors continued to come together.

5. *The exodus.* By the miracle of 20/20 hindsight, the decision to move from institution to house churches appears to have been a colossal mistake. In naïveté and ignorance (we thought it was faith), we believed (a) our leaders were ready to shepherd the house-church flocks; (b) our people were ready to follow the leaders into the challenging house-church form; and (c) our relationships were healthy enough to keep us together.

In spite of the extent to which we had come to believe that the church is "people-not-buildings," the property at 4640 North Granite Reef Road was clearly part of the glue that had held us together.

I have been in contact with many house churches that grew to the point where they chose to occupy a special "church building," and I know of many house churches that grew by dividing, but I know of no other institutional church that has tried to move out of its buildings in order to divide into house churches. For most people it takes a significant change in thinking about the church to make the adjustment to the loose informality of a church life built around home meetings. The O.H. family had heard much teaching concerning the nature of the church as people ministering to people, a royal priesthood that needs nothing but Jesus and one another in order to function, and how the name of Jesus Christ, not anything as institutional or worldly as church buildings, is the legitimate and biblical gathering place for the body of Christ. But it clearly needed more direction and closer shepherding than we as leaders were able to provide without the "corral effect" of a building into which to gather the flock.

7. *The sovereign working of God.* Bob Betts, a young man in his thirties who came to Christ and Our Heritage while still in high school and went with us through the years of change (including the house-church stage), said to me, "O.H. was beyond you, Bob." He meant that it was a work of God. More happened there than could ever be credited to any man's leadership or ministry.

I think I was aware of that even while it was happening. Especially when letters came from around the globe telling how the Spirit of God was bringing many church leaders and congregations to the same conclusions about the church, based on the same Scriptures and leading to the same vision for renewal. Whatever was happening at O.H. was also happening in other places to a lot of unconnected people at the same time. This seemed to me an affirmation that what we were involved in was a work of God, a true revival.

There was life. Divine life. As weak as we were, God was doing something special with us. His own work. Something beyond mere human production. As Isaiah said,

> LORD, *you* establish peace for us; all that we have accomplished *you* have done for us (Isa. 26:12, italics added).

Does this also mean that God arranged for the church to fail? If so, why? Were our weaknesses so irreparable, so bad, that God had no choice but to lead us into destruction? Or is Mary Lazear correct in saying, "O.H. was disassembled because God needed us to go different places and *live* what we were taught"? Is the scattered influence of our renewed people that much more valuable to the work of God than the continuing demonstration of life in a living congregation?

As I struggle with these questions, I remember what happened in Jerusalem circa A.D. 40. That church had been dynamite! Their growth is told in Acts 1 through 7, from 120 waiting for the Holy Spirit in the upper room (1:15) to 3,000 (2:41) to 5,000 (4:4) to multiplication (6:7). By Acts 8, their numbers were in five figures. And what a fellowship it was! One brief description gives us a taste:

> All the believers were one in heart and mind. No one claimed that any of his possessions was his own, but they shared everything they had. With great power the apostles continued to testify to the resurrection of the Lord Jesus, and much grace was upon them all. There were no needy persons among them. For from time to time those who owned lands and houses sold them, brought the money from the sales and put it at the apostles' feet and it was distributed to anyone as he had need (Acts 4:32–35).

As Larry Richards would say, "Millennial!"

It was the kind of close, caring, and successful church fellowship we dream about. The church in Acts experienced it. And would have stayed with it "till death do us part" had Saul of Tarsus not gone on his wild rampage (Acts. 8:1–3). He all but annihilated the church in Jerusalem. Believers leaped out of their once-cozy spiritual nest and ran for their lives. The church at Jerusalem was scattered. Dissolved. Wrecked. Down for the count. Gone.

I want to blame Saul. But as I read on, I see the hidden hand of the Almighty, like a brilliant military strategist deploying his troops to get them into the best positions for conquest.

> Those who had been scattered preached the word wherever they went (Acts 8:4).

Dynamic little "Jerusalem-style" churches sprang up wherever the seed of the gospel was scattered as dispersing Christians shared and lived what they had been taught.

Is Mary Lazear right? Is this what God was doing with our church? It doesn't answer all my questions, but it gives a measure of peace. Whatever the cause of our dispersion, God is using the people where they are. None that I know of has been lost to the body of Christ. Most are thriving and continuing to grow.

Notes

1. The story of the transition to house churches is told in the epilogue of my book *Brethren, Hang Together* (Grand Rapids: Zondervan, 1979), 325–30.
2. The nonbiblical names in this journal entry have been changed.

Chapter 4

If I Had It to Do Over

It is not sufficient that we seek hereafter to build up,
according to Scriptural doctrines, a good, earnest
church as men reckon it. No, *light* is our cry. We
dare to face the light. "Lord, give me, like Stephen,
to see the Son of man in heaven and in his light to
see what thy Church is; thy work is. And then, grant
me grace not only to live and walk, but also to work,
in that light!"   —*Watchman Nee*[1]

FROM EARLY CHILDHOOD I have been taught about how to
know the will of God. My spiritual tutors said that potential
decisions should always be tested against (1) the Word of God,
(2) conscience (the inner sense of right and wrong), (3) the
advice of godly people, and (4) the "open doors" (opportunity). At times we may be called of God to do the thing that our
peers, worldly and Christian, do not feel is wise or prudent. In
which case, we are usually moved to action by an unrelenting

sense that the thing *must be done*, that God will be displeased if it is not. This compelling sense is what my teachers called "conviction."

The decision to give our church building to our denomination and to move our congregation out into house churches seemed to erupt from the flames of rekindled aspiration and deepened trust in each other. We had talked about it for years, never sure when or if ever we would make the move. Together our five elders had already led the church through significant structural changes. In the fall, four of the five spent a week on retreat with leaders of seven other churches. There we broke through to a new level of harmony and a new clarity of vision for the church. We kept in touch with the fifth elder through daily phone calls. Upon our return all five met together, with our wives, to share the impact of that week and to discuss its implications. Almost immediately the ten of us knew: *Now is the time! This is the will of God for us and our congregation.* We were certain we were hearing the voice of the Holy Spirit.

Looking back, I can see what I was incapable of seeing then—that we were not ready to make the move we made. I was not ready, and our leaders were grossly unprepared to shepherd the flock in its new configuration. But by all the tests, this was the will of God for us—it was biblical, it was not sinful, it was affirmed by a trusted cadre of godly men and women, and the door seemed wide open. The inner conviction that we must do it was both compelling and exhilarating.

When we announced the plan to the congregation, a few expressed caution, but all seemed willing and ready to follow their shepherds into the new form.

And house churches were not a novelty. They have existed throughout ecclesiastical history. Special buildings for Christian meetings were not commonplace until the fourth century. The New Testament records the existence of many house churches, known only by the names of the people in whose homes they met. Contemporary house churches in many parts of the world were known to us. We were convinced that the Holy Spirit was calling us to provide a model.

Today, even though hard experience has made me wiser, more cautious, and more aware of potential problems, if I felt with a group of trusted Christian friends the same compelling unanimity of conviction that the elders at Our Heritage experienced together in the fall of 1978, I would join them in that conviction, no matter how risky or radical the action seemed.

Yes . . . I'd do it again!

To some, such an admission may seem foolish in light of all the tragedy that followed. Why expose myself to all that risk? The answer lies in the value of the treasure sought. For me, to live within the church as Jesus described it is a privilege and a necessity worth any risk.

Sometimes when I consider the bold, powerful style of church life of which Jesus and the apostles make us dream, I get angry. I find it impossible not to compare the community he talks about with the church as most of us are experiencing it today. And quite frankly, I feel ripped off—as if something I have been promised has been stolen from me before I had a chance to touch it! In its place cruel robbers have left a lifeless, musty, unhappy, and unblessed substitute for the rich inheritance that is rightfully mine.

MY GRANDFATHER'S GOLD WATCH

When my grandfather died, he left his magnificent, old railroad watch to me in his will. It was solid gold with an engraved cover that snapped shut. It had dangled from a fob that hung in an inverted leathern arc across the old man's stomach. I was twelve years old at the time of his death. The watch was to be given to me at my eighteenth birthday.

In the meantime, my father carried it and used it. Every time I saw him take it out of his pocket to check the time, I thought, "That watch is mine." I felt proud and anticipated the day when it would actually come into my possession. But before I could reach eighteen, the watch wore out. I don't remember what happened to it. I never got to carry it, even though it was mine by inheritance and promise from my grandfather.

My experience with the church has been a lot like that. The disappointment is so great that at times it seems unbearable.

When Jesus died, the new community of salt, light, and life he had spent his life to establish was bequeathed to me (to all of us) as an inheritance. Nearly two thousand years later I became a Christian. The inheritance supposedly became mine. Since then, I've been searching for it among the remains of the church. To my mortification I discovered that in the time between the death of the Testator and my new birth, the wonderful earthly community he described and the early disciples lived has gone woefully amuck! It has become bogged down in the mire of myriad worldly attachments and ten thousand antiquated and confusing human traditions. The society Jesus left was snatched from me and misused and mutilated before I ever came of age! I have never experienced it. I can only read about it . . . and weep.

THE NEW TESTAMENT CHURCH STILL BECKONS

Only the coldest soul fails to thrill to the story of the ecclesiological phenomenon of Acts 2.

Three thousand were baptized in a single day. Immediately they became part of a life-changing body of believers who gathered daily to hear the apostles' teaching concerning Jesus and to cling to one another, share with one another, and remember the Lord's death in the breaking of bread. How they prayed! Awe-inspiring evidence of spiritual reality filled their experience together, including miracles. It was a high thing just to be together! They knew each other—including personal and family needs—and they took material as well as spiritual responsibility for each other. How they cared! Every day they were together somewhere—on the temple porch, in one another's homes, meeting, sharing, eating meals together, rejoicing together, praising God together. And nothing was "put on" or affected—it was all real! Even nonbelievers watched and recognized that what was happening was genuine and good. Every day the addition of new believers marked this as a work of God (Acts 2:41–47).

When the Holy Spirit invaded the lives of Jesus' friends, among the resulting signs and wonders was *the church!*

For most of us, life in the church has been so lifeless, tradition-encrusted, and man-made that it seems unbelievable that the corporate Christian experience could ever have been so wonderful. Perhaps it was a fluke. An accident of history. A radiant episode never intended to happen again. Or the model of some future millennial experience hung in front of us like the proverbial carrot to keep the proverbial jackass moving.

No! None of these explanations will do. This was church as Jesus Christ, the Head of the church, intended it to be.

There is a simple explanation for the "unusual" turn of events in Jerusalem. One has only to reread the record of what Jesus of Nazareth had been saying and demonstrating for three and one-half years. The Sermon on the Mount in Matthew 5–7, for example. And the instructions he gave for the apostolic training missions in Matthew 10 and Luke 10. And the challenges to all-out discipleship in Luke 6 and 12. What made the church experience of the original believers so unique was the simple fact that they were obeying the teaching of Jesus. Never mind that these teachings were unbelievably radical. When the personal energy of Jesus Christ was in them because of the Holy Spirit, in their naïveté (or was it faith?) they simply had no other strategy in mind but the one he had given them.

Did the Jerusalem Three Thousand give high priority to teaching? (See Acts 2:42.) Their model was the strong didactic ministry of the Master Teacher. He had promised them that when they had learned their lessons well they would be exactly like their teacher (Luke 6:40).

Did they eat simple meals together and remember the Lord at mealtime? (See Acts 2:46.) Jesus repeatedly disclosed his splendor at mealtime, from the feeding of the five thousand to the Last Supper to the unveiling at Emmaus. When he sent the disciples out a-preaching the good news of the kingdom, he told them to expect to share meals with those who believed their word (Matt. 10:11; Luke 10:7).

Did they pray? (See Acts 2:42.) Jesus taught them how (Matt. 6:5–15). His prayer life was so powerful and consistent, it became an inescapable model for them. When his Spirit filled them, their "automatic" response was to pray.

Did they experience visible evidences (signs) of spiritual reality? (See Acts 2:43.) What were they to expect but that their experience with him in the flesh would continue to be their experience with him in the Spirit? Signs and wonders filled his days. And he gave them clear instructions about their mission: "Heal the sick, raise the dead, cleanse the lepers, drive out demons" (Matt. 10:8).

Was what happened among them cause for near-breathless worship and excited acknowledgment of God's working? (See Acts 2:43, 46–47.) Such awe was nothing new for people who had been going around for three years with their mouths hanging open in sheer wonder at the Lord.

Were all the believers together? Did they share everything in common? Did they sell their possessions in order to give something to needy brothers? (See Acts 2:44–45.) This seems so foreign to the modern church experience, so surprising, so imprudent! Though we have read him and heard him preached for years, many of us have never yet really *heard* Jesus saying . . .

> Watch out! Be on your guard against all kinds of greed; a man's life does not consist in the abundance of his possessions (Luke 12:15).

> Do not be afraid, little flock, for your Father has been pleased to give you the kingdom. *Sell your possessions and give to the poor.* Provide purses for yourselves that will not wear out, a treasure . . . that will not be exhausted (Luke 12:32–33, italics added).

They had heard him say it.

Some insist that the Jerusalem church's way of doing things is impractical for all but smaller churches. When a church gets bigger, they say, it needs more direction and more regulation. Helping ministries must become more formal, less spontaneous and personal, more institutionalized as the church grows. Acts 6 certainly indicates that there is a place for increasing organizational oversight to make sure that all the needy are cared for. But if spontaneous and sacrificial personal sharing really are impractical in the larger church, then every large church should be divided into smaller units until these things become "practical" again.

The fact is, the church at Jerusalem was no little church. There were 3,120 of them living together in that radical *koinonia* at first. Within two years the number grew to 10,000. Growth did not change their strategy. Their program was still as simple as *trying to do what Jesus had told them to do.* When they did, the book of Acts happened.

Since those simple-but-wonderful days, the church has had nineteen and one-half centuries to discover "better" ways to do things.

Today, every weekend millions of Christians gather to hear what God has to say without the slightest intention of actually practicing most of what they hear. Most of us are what James was afraid we'd be—*hearers of the Word, but not doers* (James 1:22–25). The more we hear without doing, the more deeply rooted becomes the habit. This is why going to another church service or listening to another sermon is not going to make most of us better Christians.

The church in most people's experience does not set its priorities or pattern its life after the priorities and life modeled in Scripture. We're too sophisticated for such simplicity. Instead, we've gathered our wisdom from secular organizations, education, psychology, business, public opinion polls, and church tradition. And then we have convinced ourselves that the Word of God is either silent on such things or that it agrees with us. We do what we want: meeting, relating to one another, and carrying on the work of the church according to our own priorities, ideas, preferences, habits, and what is most compatible with secular society, as though God had left the driving to us.

Some of us have accommodated ourselves to a religious

status quo in which Acts 2 is seen as a misty legend, an allegory at best; certainly not a glimmer of hope for anything that might actually happen in today's church. Others look at the first part of Acts 2 and seek ecstatic experiences with the Holy Spirit, but never get to the last eight verses where the baptism with the Holy Spirit is evidenced in a visible, down-to-earth lifestyle in which people are cared for even if it means that the rich get poorer and the independent get involved in the costly processes that go with being a responsible member of a close-knit family. Some people never stop flitting from one spiritual "happening" to another long enough to be what Jesus told us to be to each other. One would think Jesus had told us that the world would know we are his disciples by our giddy pursuit of experiences and miracles, instead of by the way we lay down our lives for each other (John 15:12–13).

Are we doomed to choose between accommodating to a tasteless religious status quo or losing ourselves in a quest for narcissistic substitutes for spiritual reality? Or does the church in the Acts offer us more?

We are not kept from the fullness of church life because we lack the resources the early church had. The power of the Holy Spirit, the gifts, and Jesus' secrets for our life together are no less available today than then. The Head of the church is the same yesterday, today, and forever (Heb. 13:8). The problem is that little by little through the misty decades since the early days, the church stopped listening to him and so stopped thinking the way he thinks. In many places she has traded the honor of being the audacious community of Jesus for social respectability. In others she has turned spiritual power inward and made it a thing of self-gratification rather than the source of energy for self-sacrificing servanthood.

God is undeniably at work in our day, cleansing and confronting the church and calling her to return from her nauseating lukewarmness to new spiritual fire. At times we watch in amazement as he visibly brings down high things in her that have been raised up to obscure the truth, purging and cleansing away the worldly garbage that seems so attractive to some churchgoers. There are pockets where things are happening that encourage us to believe the beliefs of Jesus and to dream his dreams. But there is a definite shortage of authentic models of the spiritual community he describes.

The kind and quality of church life Jesus dares us to share together only happens among doers of his Word.

PRINCIPLES OF CHURCH LIFE

The young-to-middle-aged rebels of Our Heritage Church may have been rambunctious daredevils playing Russian roulette with the holy relics of sacred tradition. What was produced may have been far from the biblical ideal in ten thousand ways. But what we did represented a sincere attempt to find the real thing.

Label us naïve, incompetent, stubborn, careless, ignorant, stupid, dangerous, imprudent, foolish, blind, rebellious, or crazy, but don't label us cowardly or uncommitted, because those labels won't stick.

We cared about the will of God. We cared about the practical authority of Scripture to direct the church. We cared about being biblical and Spirit-led. The changes we tried to make were based on principles we discerned from study of the Scriptures. We put our lives on the line for what we thought God wanted us to do.

Our Heritage Church did not turn out to be the perpetual monument to our correctness that we would have preferred. Instead, it disintegrated and all but disappeared. Obviously something went wrong. But our apparent failure is not proof that every principle by which we were guided was wrong. Nor does it prove that all the things we were hungering for in the church were unspiritual or unrealistic.

All we knew when we started was that our church (a fairly typical urban, evangelical congregation) was in an anemic spiritual condition. There was not enough in it to make baby Christians really grow up; the priesthood of believers was barely functioning; love between the brothers and sisters was too shallow. If the description of the church in the book of Acts represents part of "the Promise of the Gospel," for us it was an unfulfilled promise.

Confronted with such gross spiritual deficiency, we decided to believe in the church the Bible tells about. We searched the Scriptures for clues as to how that church functioned as it did, principles we could pull out and apply to our failing fellowship that might turn it around.

We examined the New Testament church for its fundamentals, and as each truth emerged we asked the Lord to show us practical places in the life of our church where it might become operational. We asked him to help us face up to specific changes that each principle called for. Most changes, we came to realize, would have to be implemented in stages; few could be made instantly. But our commitment was to change the church eventually in any and every way biblical truth indicated.

After several years of searching and experimenting, we were able to identify several basic principles that we felt needed specific attention as we edged toward the New Testament ideal.[2]

Principle 1: The church is people alive in Christ.

The biblical church is not buildings (they possessed none, built none), nor programs of education (other than the meetings of the church and the sharing of personal experiences with Christ), nor public relations (other than the news that spread from mouth to mouth), nor hierarchies (the servant-facilitators who cared for the flock were in no sense lords or heads). The focus was always on people. People were the church's only inventory and product. This reality gave everything a human and relational focus. Funds were never raised for anything else. Energy was never expended for anything else. Health and strength were always measured in terms of what was happening with persons.

Principle 2: The church gathers around the person of Jesus Christ.

> "For where two or three come together in my name, there am I with them" (Matt. 18:20).
>
> And our fellowship is with the Father and with his Son, Jesus Christ (1 John 1:3).

Christ is present in his church. Everything in the life of the church revolves around him. A church where Christ is the heartbeat of the fellowship and life and, where the believer-priesthood is functioning, can be strong and effective with or without a building, a professional pastor, and many of the other things in which church people find security and enjoyment, and which sometimes become substitutes for simply sharing the Life of Christ together.

Principle 3: The church is dependent on the Holy Spirit for the ability to do and to be all that God commands.

Two vital relationships seemed to be the key to the movement of the New Testament church: (1) relationship with God, and (2) relationship between members. When their relationship with God was healthy, the people of the church were described as "filled with the Spirit." When their mutual relationships were sound, they shared *agape* (divine love) with one another. Everything good seemed to happen in the context of those two connections.

Principle 4: Jesus Christ is the present Head of the church.

Christ's leadership of his people is not merely historical; it is existential and contemporary. A group of Christians can tune in on his voice and personal directorship by paying attention to (1) what the written Word of God has to say to the church, (2) the specific spiritual gifts he has distributed among its members, and (3) the harmonious agreement (consensus) of its mature spiritual leaders. Prayer, searching the Scriptures, waiting on the Lord, and listening to each other need to be part of every church decision (Matt. 18:18–20; Acts 15:1–29).

Principle 5: The ministry of the church is by its royal priesthood, which includes all believers.

All the great edification passages in the New Testament describe the indispensable ministry of every believer, every part, and every member if the body is to grow up into the full stature of Christ (Rom. 12; 1 Cor. 12–14; Eph. 4:11–16; 5:18–21). The church will never grow up until it experiences the ministry of a wide variety of people sharing together what the Lord has given them for each other.

Principle 6: Pastoral leadership is by a team of people chosen from among the local congregation for their spiritual maturity, giftedness for ministry, and the exemplary quality of their lives.

The shepherding and care of God's flock was never intended to be the task of the Lone Ranger! Spiritual care and leadership are, in the broadest sense, given to all believers for the others and, in a specialized sense, are given to a team of "peer pastors" who serve the overall needs that only such a team can serve (Acts 14:23; 20:17–35; 1 Tim. 3; Titus 1). They are local men and women who have already been using what the Lord has given them to help the church. Their appointment as pastors (elders, overseers, bishops) serves to focus the gifts and calling that are already benefiting their brothers and sisters. The model of their lives in Christ is visible and well-known. They have the power to make Christ relevant to everyday life in the real world, because the message is not obscured by the mist of unwarranted reverential distance, which can result in treating leaders with a "pedestal mentality" that undermines the impact of example, making committed Christian living seem like "something only a preacher can do, not me."

Principle 7: The regular meetings of the church are for the maturing of believers.

If the church's meetings are always aimed at "evangelizing" the small number of unbelievers who might have dropped in, then when and where is the average Christian ever going to be exposed to anything to grow on?

Nonbelievers who come to a gathering where Christians are being taught to know who they are in Christ and who he is in them, along with the finer points of what it means to follow him as a true disciple, will be drawn toward him by the Holy Spirit. So evangelism can take place. When Christians are together, which is only a little time out of every week, their meeting needs to be calculated to bring about edification.

The teaching must be the teaching of the Scriptures, not shallow sermonizing in which the person in the pulpit shares his or her entertaining advice. Something needs to happen that makes the truth part of the listeners—a question-and-answer period following the sermon, small-group interaction, congregational feedback, even occasional debate. And others besides the leaders must be given an opportunity to respond, to share, to say what they think, to talk about what God is doing in their lives, or to ask for specific help.

Corporate praise and worship that actually involve the minds, hearts, and voices of the worshipers is needed. Participation puts into practice what is being taught.

Principle 8: Church fellowship and discipline are facilitated by the development of loving relationships.

Christ must be kept central. True Christocentricity never really happens where Christians close off to one another and see themselves as worshiping Jesus *without* loving their fellow Christians. John says you can't do that (1 John 4:20). Jesus says the thing that marks us as his is our love for one another (John 13:34–35).

The love that is the throb of real fellowship and out of which genuine care for each other emerges is love like Jesus'. It goes to the cross for its objects. It doesn't cut and run when the going gets rough. It bears the failures and sins of others. It's still there after being misunderstood, hurt, and rejected. It keeps caring. It keeps cheering for its spiritual kin. It keeps working for their spiritual benefit.

It's personal. It wants to be with its fellows. When kin are in need, it shares to meet the need.

Koinonia, the New Testament word for fellowship, embraces this concept. It denotes sharing, participation, interaction, relationship. Spiritual progress and correction are meant to take place in such a context. When confrontation, correction, and discipline must come, they come from someone who is administering what is needed out of personal relationship and self-sacrificing love.

Principle 9: Evangelism occurs when the church is healthy.

Our original expectation, based on a number of passages in the book of Acts (2:47; 6:7; 9:31; 16:15), was that individuals sharing out of the overflow of their growth in Christ would, as a matter of course, influence their world with a witness as effective as that of the New Testament church. As people become alive to Christ and aware of his daily working in their lives, they share their faith more freely and naturally. The process takes time. Training and encouragement will enhance the process in some people. Simple organizational strategies that leave individuals free to express their witness in keeping with personal giftedness may also be helpful in reaching people outside the natural circle of relationships. But in nurturing evangelism and witness, nothing can replace a life together that stimulates general health in the two key spiritual relationships—with God through his Holy Spirit, and with fellow believers sharing agape love.

Principle 10: The spiritual nurture of children is primarily the responsibility of their parents.

Nearly everything the Bible says about children in the church gives the direct responsibility for their spiritual education to the family, especially parents (Deut. 6; Eph. 6:4; 2 Tim. 1:5; 3:14–15). Sound spiritual parenting will usually produce sound spiritual offspring. The church and Sunday school are no substitutes for that. The most a congregation can do is to help. It may be appropriate for the body to provide biblical instruction for children, but the congregation should expend most if its energy toward bringing adults to Jesus and nurturing them up in him. If adults are experiencing a living faith, they will transmit it to their children.

Principle 11: All who confess the Lord Jesus Christ as Savior and Lord share the essential "unity of the Spirit" with one another.

According to the apostles, there is to be no division among Christian believers over such things as leaders, opinions, disagreements, racial and social differences, diversity of spiritual experiences, or diversity of gifts and ministries (John 17:21–26; Rom. 14; 15:1–7; 1 Cor. 1:10–13; 3:1–4; 8; 12; 13; Gal. 3:28; Eph. 2:11–18; 4:1–6; Col. 3:11; James 2:1–9). Oneness in Christ is not an experience reserved only for those who share the same religious or ethnic background, or who hold the same opinion about the meaning of every Bible passage. Oneness in Christ is experienced by those who (1) confess him as Lord, (2) recognize their essential oneness in him, (3) receive one another as Christ receives them, and (4) commit themselves to the well-being of their Christian brothers, not merely themselves.[3]

We were aware that what we had discovered was incomplete. Had we had more years together, other elements would surely have emerged and these first eleven principles would have been refined. The demise of the church seems certain evidence that we missed some fundamental truths.

A respected fellow pastor once told me, "Bob, you've taken these principles *too far!*" Perhaps he was right. At times I'm ready to admit it. We may have misapplied them often. But I cannot escape the conviction that they are nonetheless true. They still beg for practical application and corrective influence in the life of the church today.

Even though the mistakes of the past have made me wiser and the passage of time has made me more prudent, if I were faced with the same circumstances in a church and discovered the same principles in Scripture, I would be bound to pursue change, even though I know now the pain involved in such a pursuit.

Yes . . . I'd do it again!

PRINCIPLE VS. APPLICATION

One discovery tempers my present approach to church renewal: *There is a distinct difference between principle and application.* The Bible's principles cannot be compromised; but their application may vary widely according to the personality, giftedness, spiritual maturity, and specific needs of the group. The principles of Scripture are eternal and infallible; but our personal grasp and application of them can be as flawed as we are.

I have not found it easy to tell the difference. Sometimes at Our Heritage we were ready to die for our application procedures as well as for God's truths. Much damage was done. Losses were suffered that might have been unnecessary.

The Lord may wish to give his people more time to adjust than we are willing to give them. He gave the Jerusalem church nearly forty years to make the changes in the corporate wineskin that the new wine demanded. During those four decades (A.D. 33 to 70), Hebrew Christians clung to their old patterns of worship and religious association while moving gradually into the new patterns that would eventually replace them. Their dependence on the ancient observances would have to end. Change would have to come. But the Lord waited patiently for it. He ultimately allowed rejection and persecution by their countrymen to push them the last necessary steps toward freedom from the old and full experience of the new.

Participation in the old-style worship did not end for Christian Jews until just before the fall of Jerusalem, when, in an intense wave of persecution, they were excommunicated from the temple. The letter to the Hebrews was written to assure them that they could get along without the temple and old covenant practices because Christ had fulfilled them all, rendering them obsolete. An entire generation had to pass from the scene before the transition could be completed.

Ignorance of his ways and pride in our own ways made us at O.H. impatient, too much in a hurry. Perhaps we confused unchangeable principles with a flexible timetable.

A FAILED BUT NOT FORGOTTEN DREAM

To some, what happened at Our Heritage may have seemed an irreverent "affair," a clandestine excursion into the bed of a long-lost childhood sweetheart, an act of unfaithfulness to the legitimate wife of status quo denominationalism. To us it was a chaste love affair with the Spirit-inspired dream of the authentic church. It was a dream never fully realized, a dream apparently lost.

But our dream of a renewed church was based on the New Testament ideal as we perceived it. In many ways, human nature being what it is, it was probably an unrealistic dream. Being who we were, it was spiritually beyond us.

But because it has its ultimate roots in Scripture and not in our fantasies or immaturity, the dream is not dead. The aspiration that moved us was divine. The flame of hope for the church still blazes up in our hearts. Even the most dismal aspects of our failure cannot put it out.

Given another chance, a fresh start, a new day, and a few childlike souls willing to dream and experiment with us, we are compelled to try again to capture the vision ignited by the New Testament church.

Notes

1. Watchman Nee, *What Shall This Man Do?* (Fort Washington, Pa.: Christian Literature Crusade, 1967), 85.
2. Robert C. Girard, *Brethren, Hang Loose* (Grand Rapids: Zondervan, 1972), 80–91; and *Brethren, Hang Together* (Grand Rapids: Zondervan, 1979), 331.
3. *Bylaws of Montezuma Chapel*, 1987. Article V, "The Unity of the Church," 2.

Chapter 5

Is There Life After Failure?

Lord, I want your heart to be my heart. For in You I come alive, moving ahead from boring death to exciting life!

In Your promises, I will move from discouragement to hope.

In Your pardon, I will move from shame to glory.

In Your power, I will move from weakness to strength.

In Your providence, I will move from failure to success! Thank You, Lord.

Amen.

—*Robert H. Schuller*[1]

DISCOURAGED OVER multiplying failures, I saw my life as an endless flow of trash. I seemed unable to make anything go right. Depression hung like landfill stench out of what seemed a decade of failure and hopelessness. One gloomy day I turned to the Psalms. I have learned to count on the Bible musicians to tell the truth and to be coming from the same kind of feeling place I live in. Something in Psalm 113 told me God knew exactly where I was. There was hope.

> He raiseth up the poor out of the dust, and lifteth the needy out of the dunghill; That he may set him with princes . . . (Ps. 113:7–8, KJV).

I showed the passage to Audrey.

"Look!" I said, "God says he is going to lift me out of this garbage and make me a prince!"

Life on the dunghill and life in the palace are vastly different. The stench clings even when one leaves the dump for an occasional foray into the city. Even baths fail to clear the nostrils and cleanse the palate. A whiff of fresh air passing through olfactory senses saturated with dung stench still smells the same—the whole world is a dunghill! Add to this the strangling fumes of humiliation and failed hope. More paralyzing, the dunghill squatter finds security in his paper hovel and the piles of other people's trash that surround him. He's hooked on it. Down inside he begins to identify with his environment. Escape from the dunghill becomes only a fading, impossible dream. Eventually he ceases to hope that he might dwell where he wants–instead of where cruel fate has forced him. Self-respect and freedom are lost.

The most wonderful advantage enjoyed by the prince is his sovereignty. He is in control of his destiny. He is free to choose. He has the resources to build his palace wherever he wants, even high on some pleasing mountain where the air is clean and the old life on the dunghill only occasionally crosses his mind. Even when he visits the squatters to try to help another get free, he never loses his own freedom; the chains of poverty and failure never weigh him down. Even when in love he manacles himself for the sake of another, he never forgets who he is and that his father is the king. He identifies with royalty, even while empathizing with those still caught in the dunghill's ghetto. He is growing. His world is expanding. Life is getting bigger and better. He is learning to reign.

With God there is always a place to begin again. When forgiveness and grace are applied to the past, we find ourselves in the sunrise of a new dawn. I may have blown it royally yesterday, but the moment I turn to him, I get a fresh start. All that remains of yesterday's bitter defeat is a better grip on reality and God. I can build anew on that. And what is built is more likely to stand.

Cut loose from my pastoral responsibilities after my resignation, I felt free to look to the future. "What am I going to be when I grow up?" I asked. (I was forty-seven years old.) God knows that my heart was saying, "Lord, what do you want me to do with the pieces that are left of my life?"

We had been planning to build a home in Scottsdale, near two of the O.H. families with whom our lives had been entwined. We had put money down on a lot and had applied for building permits and financing. The titling process uncovered a snag that delayed the project for five months, time for some intensive searching for God's next step and discovery of a new direction.

During that time I was undergoing primal therapy and getting to know my true feelings about many things, including the real reasons for choosing the site for our home. I discovered that while genuine love for and commitment to our dear friends played a part, a lot of unfounded guilt was also connected with the choice. I could find no personal peace until the decision was made to build elsewhere.

"If not Scottsdale, where?" was the next logical question.

The only piece of property we owned in the entire world was a small lot (a gift) in the Verde Valley town of Lake Montezuma, a hundred miles north of Scottsdale. We had visited the spot a couple of times during the years, flown a kite from it, and daydreamed about developing it into a place where the family could get away from time to time. Our daydreams never included permanent residence.

But now Audrey and I heard ourselves asking, "What about building in Lake Montezuma?"

We drove to the top of the mesa and walked around

among the cactus, beargrass, and mesquite. It was a lovely place. There was plenty of open space between the handful of houses scattered here and there. The sky was clear and uncluttered. The wind blew fresh against our faces. Desert mountains rose on all the horizons. The quiet enveloped us like a soft, cool comforter. We could feel the tension easing away from our city-weary bodies.

"It's so pleasant up here," one of us said to the other, "but wouldn't it be even better if our lot was near the edge of the mesa—a 'view lot'?"

God worked in the life of two friends, Jules and Beth Klagge, to turn our heart's desire into miraculous reality.

We had lived in parsonages nearly all our adult lives, so we did not own a home. Aside from a gift from Audrey's brother and one from someone at O.H., we had no savings with which to build, and inflation was sending the cost of construction materials sky-high. We were living on a minimal income from Audrey's teaching at Scottsdale Christian Academy, my on-again-off-again writing, and my part-time filling station job.

Out of the blue came a check for seven hundred dollars from a Christian acquaintance who said simply that the Lord had told him to send it to us.

Audrey suggested, "God is going to help us build a house at a time when we have the least money and the costs of building are the highest."

We did not know when we would make the move, but the conviction was growing that we would eventually live there.

On one of our early visits to the Verde Valley, Audrey had visited Beaver Creek School, the local elementary school, to check employment possibilities. Months later, the principal called to ask if she would be available to teach the coming school year. But Audrey had already signed her contract for another year at the academy and neither of us felt it was the right time for Beaver Creek.

We visited the little community church and, though the formality was a change from the "hang-loose" house-church atmosphere we were used to, we were pleased to hear the pastor preaching a simple, straightforward gospel message. We felt strangely "at home." "If there's any life in that church," we had said, "when we move there, we'll join it." It seemed like another confirmation of our growing conviction.

In the spring of 1981, Scottsdale Christian Academy gave its teachers their contracts to sign as usual. My filling station job had ended, and I was winding up several months of intensive research for a novel I was writing. Audrey and I were sitting on the bench in front of our rental house in North Phoenix, watching the Arizona sun go down.

"I can't see myself teaching at SCA another year," she said.

"I can't see us living here another year," I said.

"I don't know if there are any teaching openings in Lake Montezuma."

"And I don't have any income prospects, other than this writing—which the publisher may not accept."

Where would we live? Audrey could withdraw the money from her teachers' retirement fund—two thousand dollars. We would ask God to provide us with a secondhand mobile home for that amount of money. We would live in that while God helped us build the house.

We would also be dependent on him to provide our daily bread. The prospects were both invigorating and scary.

Audrey would contact Beaver Creek School to see if there were any openings. I would keep writing. With or without assurance of support, when the school year ended we would pack up our goods and head for the country. We both knew: it was time to move. Peace accompanied the decision. It felt strange; we were doing exactly what we *wanted* to do.

"WHAT IS YOUR SUPPORT BASE?"

I seldom sleep without dreaming.

Not long after our arrival in our new setting, as the process of sorting out the meanings of the wrenching experiences of the past few years continued, I had a dream. I recall no details except for the question that was repeated at least a dozen times in the course of the dream: "What is your support base?"

Half awake, half asleep, I struggled to answer the question. It seemed to be calling for an evaluation of the forces that had carried me through the years of failure upon failure upon failure: the collapse of my work, the disintegration of the church, the disintegration of my emotional foundations, the breakdown of lifelong relationships, the strain on home and marriage—all the embarrassments, reverses, and falls that had pushed me to the edge of suicide, apostasy, and hopelessness. What had sustained me? Why was I still alive? What had kept me afloat when I should have drowned? Where did the stability come from to make it through the great lifequake that could have wiped me out along with those around me?

In the twilight zone between dream and reality, I felt compelled to answer. Upon waking up I wrote down five reasons why I'm still here to take advantage of the new chance grace has opened up. Men have made it off the dunghill without some of these things, but God knew I needed them all!

AUDREY

I've never known anybody quite like Audrey. I was captured by her unique personal strength, simple faith, and farm-girl naïveté one weekend when we sang duets as part of a Christian college gospel team. After that weekend, before our first date, I told a friend that she was the girl I would marry. I was certain God approved. All that remained was to court and convince Audrey.

Seven months later, we were married.

She has proven herself capable of an awesome tenacity of commitment. Partly, I have chided, it's hardheaded Danish stubbornness inherited from her farmer-father. But Audrey cannot be explained without understanding her great capacity for tough, impeccable loyalty and love. She can forgive and forget the direst husbandly foibles overnight. She simply refuses to give up. She possesses amazing self-discipline, which she uses to act out love even in the face of extreme difficulty.

At the same time Audrey feels intensely. When my pain was the greatest, even though I often took it out on her, she became aggressively passionate, comforting me and sealing our relationship more tightly. She hurts deeply and cares instinctively and genuinely. She has a crusader's sense of injustice. She fumes over women who flirt. An inveterate mother hen, she is ready to spread her wings over unprotected children and adults whenever she sees a storm coming.

Since age thirteen when she met Jesus, Audrey has experienced a sense of spiritual reality in her walk with God that in some ways is quite mystical. On lonely pastoral walks as a teenager, she communed with him and heard him speak to her. She was surprised to learn that not every Christian experiences such intimacy. In her adulthood, intimacy with God has translated into an almost immediate certainty about his will and a well-developed capacity to discern truth from error, good from evil, false from real. Often she is saying, "This is what God wants us to do," while I'm still trying to decipher his signals.

Audrey gets special insights ("words from the Lord") concerning problems and situations. Conflicts come when I am not hearing the same thing. But as we struggled through the hard times I've been describing, and our relationship sometimes became painfully strained, and inner conflicts erupted into bitter and confusing exchanges, she often would be given an insight in the midst of the crises. The Holy Spirit seemed to whisper a secret that would clear up the confusion and give her hope that God was working in spite of the apparent wreckage of our landscape.

Because she is what she is, has the clear relationship with God that she has, and chooses to love as she does, there has always been stability in our home, even when my instability would have torn it apart.

As I began to emerge from the primal therapy, to put behind me my failures in relationships and ministry, and to ask, "Where do I go from here? What do I do with my life now?" Audrey made a new kind of commitment to me and our marriage.

"I will work to provide a roof over our heads and food on the table," she said, "if you will find out what you really want to do and do it."

She meant it.

I owe Audrey the survival of our home and the freedom I now have to pick up the pieces and pursue my dreams. Without her I could have gotten lost at any of a hundred danger points and fallen over some unalterable precipice.

THE FAMILY

What an advantage to go through the stuff of life surrounded and supported by a family that closes ranks when trouble comes! When everything else seemed to be coming down around my ears, my family was there and weathered the hurricane.

Audrey and I traveled through dangerous times, but love and commitment always kept us coming back to each other's arms. In the final analysis, there was nowhere else either of us ever wanted to be.

In the midst of it all, our children were great! Given their father's instability, they had many of the reasons other kids have for rebelling against their parents and God, for giving up, dropping out, or losing faith. But they didn't. Even though they were sometimes confused by what was going on in the home, they were faithful, respectful, and obedient. They clung tightly together and kept loving both God and their parents, and they said so often.

During the "comeback years," the failure-and-guilt syndrome would return at times to haunt me. Depression and discouragement would set in. Then the kids would come home for Thanksgiving or Christmas or just to be home—and suddenly life was filled with fresh evidence that all was not lost, that something in my life actually worked. Someone had done something right with these kids. As a father, I had been weak and struggling, but my kids were not a sign of failure!

The backbone and infrastructure of this family have been, as I've already said, the commitment of Audrey as a wife and mother to her brood. It has cost her dearly (emotionally and physically) to be strong, but we would never have survived without her firmness and love.

And even in the midst of the worst of times, our three children have been a source of parental joy. Rebelliousness was minimal—no more than the healthy stretching and growing of young individuals discovering the right sort of independence. Each has always been ready, eager, to express love. Each has pursued excellence in some special area and has brought pride to a daddy's heart: Christine, academician, musician, composer, excellent wife and mother; Bob II, top high school athlete, Christian musician, composer, dreamer (like his father); Charity Joy, top scholar, actress, drum major, "the joy of my old age." I could not be prouder of them all!

Most importantly, each one has grown to beautiful adulthood. Each has moved beyond parental faith to his or her own vital, personal relationship with the Lord. Each manifests the treasure of sterling Christian character.

To me as a parent that feels like success and prosperity.

THE BODY

I thought I knew the body of Christ before my descent into the hell of failure and weakness, but I know it even better now, because I have experienced the body's power at times when I could give it little or nothing and instead found myself completely dependent on my fellow members. During the comeback years I have experienced four powerful expressions of Christ's body.

The church family at Our Heritage accepted me at my weakest, gave me freedom to be inadequate and needy, helped me to face up to my spiritual sickness, gave me time away from church responsibilities to heal, and continued to affirm and support me (financially and emotionally) as I moved toward healing. It was an act of heroism. Many churches reject the pastor who shows them his clay feet. But this church, through the years we had trudged into love together, had learned to wrap her arms around broken people. She did not always know what to do with them but to love and stand by them, yet she understood she was there to be a refuge for strugglers. I had helped bring her to such a place. At last I found myself desperately needing the caring family she had become.

The little house-church group in Paradise Valley called itself "Grace." It had come into being as a "daughter church" sponsored jointly by O.H. and the denominational district. Jay Klagge, the pastor, had become a Christian in the early days at O.H.; his wife, Mary, had been the first teenager to receive the Lord through our ministry there. So we were not far from "home" when we decided to be part of Grace. "I need to be ministered to," I told them. "Don't expect me to give much." They took us in, accepting us as listeners, worshipers, and friends. They expected nothing. Their love wrapped around us like a soft, pure, gauze bandage, giving open wounds protection and breathing room—time to heal.

The only church in town when we arrived in Lake Montezuma was housed in a little brown A-frame structure called "Montezuma Chapel." This group of mostly retired folks welcomed us, knowing nothing of what we had been through. It was a totally different church experience from anything we had known for more than a decade and a half. Soon we knew we were being loved and accepted and needed by people who in general had little concept of the vital role they were playing in my process of recovery.

Most considered themselves Christians, but few saw themselves as especially spiritual. Some were ignorant of the meaning of terms like "saved" and "born again." Few knew their way around the Bible. They expected little. They demanded little. They loved much. And they appreciated me back into the ministry. They gave me freedom to ease back at a pace my jagged emotions could handle.

We named our house "Ebenezer." It's the name Samuel gave to a rock he had set on end as a memorial to the Lord after a glorious victory over the Philistines (1 Sam. 7:12). It means "rock of the Lord's help." I have to include it among expressions of the body of Christ because building it was a "body life" experience. Without the blessing, support, gifts, loans, instruction, advice, and physical labor of neighbors, friends, relatives, and even strangers, most of whom were Christians, we would not be enjoying the wonderful country home God gave us when we had the least money and the cost of building was the highest. Wherever we stand in this house, whatever direction we look, our eyes fall on specific evidences of the vitality and wonder of the Lord's living body.

Among the most powerful forces sustaining us in the comeback years has been the wonderful, multifaceted body Christ put together for just such a mission.

THE BIBLE

In the throes of primal therapy's unmasking process, the only book I could read was the Bible. Stories of Jesus casting out evil spirits, James' passionate exhortation to repentance (James 4:7–10), and David's penitent quest for "truth in the inward part" (Ps. 51) gave me peace.

Again and again, in the middle of the darkest times of defeat, at the point on the comeback trail where fear and doubt threatened to ravage hope, or when some new failure screamed that nothing had really changed, a burst of light from the Word of God, read or remembered, would bring essential perspective and rekindle belief in God's working. Like morning sun, some part of the Bible (a psalm, a promise, a clear bit of instruction) would turn the dark moment into broad daylight, dispelling confusion and blindness.

When my back is against the wall, when the boredom of repetitious pain or weekly pastoral deadlines makes life a drudgery, when I hunger for more of God and he seems out of focus, when I am lonely, wounded, confused, guilty, afraid, pressed, and sick at heart, I go to the Scriptures. God almost always speaks to me through them. Nearly every page has something that is surprisingly relevant to what's happening in my life.

GOD AT THE CORE

My feelings sometimes told me God was far, far away. My guilt insisted he had forsaken me. My weakness nagged that he found me disgusting. But when truth was disclosed and sanity restored, I knew he was there.

In pain and terror-driven rage, I had screamed at him. Blamed him. Cursed him. "Where are you when I need you?" Turned my back and tried to walk out on him. Determined to prove to him that I was as bad as he thought I was. Tested his forgiveness and acceptance with willful sin. And when I turned around to see where he was . . . *he was there.* Smiling a sad and knowing smile.

I tried not to believe in him. I consciously went through the process of throwing out everything I believed. It was all up for grabs. Maybe, after all these years of "serving God," he did not really exist. If that were true, my whole life had been a colossal waste of time! What had I to show for twenty-seven years of "Christian service"? Failure. Bitterness. Inner torment of guilt and fear. I would, henceforth, not believe any more.

But I could not bring it off.

When I had mentally peeled off all the layers of tradition and religion and doctrine and belief, I was left with the inescapable conviction that God was the only thing that could possibly make sense out of this world and my own life. Without him there was really no reason to go on living. Without him the world and human existence and history and the future were meaningless—they simply could not be! Without him, life would be hopeless madness far beyond anything I had experienced. If God is not there, blowing one's brains out makes sense.

God was there! I could not shake him, forget him, or

ignore him. I had to have him. He was the core of my being and person. He was everywhere. He was life. And he was everything good in life. Even Audrey, the family, the body, the Word, my own breath, my capacity to feel pain and hope—all were gifts that I could not have without him.

Just knowing he's there dissipates the stench of the dunghill. In that knowledge we catch a whiff of the clean, free air of the promised princedom.

Notes

1. Robert H. Schuller, *Success Is Never Ending, Failure Is Never Final* (Nashville: Nelson, 1988), 244.

Chapter 6

Called to Live

Most of my life has been built around the idea that my value depends on what I do. I made it through school. I earned my degrees and awards and I made my career. Yes, with many others, I fought my way up to a little success, a little popularity and a little power. But . . . how violent that journey was. So marked by rivalry and competition, so pervaded with compulsion and obsession, so spotted with moments of suspicion, jealousy, resentment and revenge.

Oh sure, most of what I did was called ministry, the ministry of justice and peace, the ministry of forgiveness and reconciliation, the ministry of healing and wholeness. But when those who want peace are as interested in success, popularity and power as those who want war, what then is the real difference between war and peace?　　　　—*Henri Nouwen*[1]

MY PROPOSED BOOK on "healing" had been turned down by a second publisher. I sat at our rickety old picnic table under the juniper tree and held the rejection letter in my hand. The view provided an automatic lift to my drooping spirit—the steep cliffside dropping off into a green valley dotted with homes, the red rocks of Oak Creek Canyon lending a pink prettiness to the northwest horizon, dark Mingus Mountain rising eight thousand feet above the valley to the west, completing the ruggedness of the terrain to provide an Old West feeling of freedom. I knew I could pursue the writing anyway and submit it to another publisher and still another until someone agreed to buy it. That's what writers have to do sometimes. But that thought seemed unthinkable for two reasons:

1. Who was I to write a book about *healing?* While many of the concepts I wanted to share were fresh and needed, I was barely well myself.

2. I was taking the publisher's refusal very personally: I felt it as personal rejection of my work by God.

I thumbed through my NIV New Testament looking for something to provide perspective. I needed to write what I was feeling in order to get my thoughts and feelings organized. My journal had been misplaced in the move from Phoenix.

The little leatherbound testament contained several blank sheets in back, so I decided to jot down a few thoughts there, which I dated and captioned "Insights out of the Struggle." (Like most of my journaling, it is mostly prayer.)

Insight 1: I know I am not rejected by God. And yet my automatic emotions project on him the "rejection" of others.

I desperately needed a word from God on this. My testament lay open at Luke 17:3–6.

> *"If your brother sins, rebuke him, and if he repents, forgive him. If he sins against you seven times in a day, and seven times comes back to you and says, 'I repent,' forgive him."*
>
> *The apostles said to the Lord, "Increase our faith!"*

He replied, "If you have faith as small as a mustard seed, you can say to this mulberry tree, 'Be uprooted and planted in the sea,' and it will obey you."

Forgive and forgive and forgive. If that seems hard, believe God. And the tree of resentment (unforgiveness) will be uprooted by faith.

Insight 2: Live! Just live!

My books are to be strictly secondary to living life and being with people and walking with God.

That's always been the message, hasn't it, friend? It was the same word you gave me in Hawaii. I thought I'd gone there to write "Brethren, Hang Together." Actually you had sent Audrey and I there to be involved in the painful struggles of two people you cared more about than my book. And I think you gave me the same message while I was trying to write the other books.

I guess I fight it because, in my unhealed view, the thing I do that gives me importance is my writing. I cling to and fight for it as though it were not merely something I do, but part of me as a person.

But you are so damn persistent. Pardon me, Lord—so "blessedly" persistent. (The second statement reflects good theology, but the first reflects more accurately the intensity of my feelings.) You will not leave me unhealed. I must see my personhood in you, Jesus, and you, Father. I must learn to credit myself with value . . . apart from anything that I do or can produce. I must reject the thinking pattern of my youth (no doubt, one of the "sins of my youth," Ps. 25:7) that grants me worth only on the basis of perfect accomplishment. And I must forgive those whose "rejection" (as I perceived it in my immaturity) led me into such a diabolical pattern of thinking.

You love me and accept me. (My secret fears deny it, but the Scriptures affirm it and Christ's death for me most profoundly proves it, Rom. 5:8.) I know your acceptance is on the basis of the cross, not my performance!

So . . . I must live. Just live, first. I must go on writing, but stop thinking that I shall make my living as a writer. I will walk by faith in you. You will supply my living through whatever means make sense. I will concentrate on getting my act together. And upon being a man—a

*man of God. The books, if I understand this concept correctly, will
come as an overflow and adjunct.*

I am to concentrate on living.

*Easier said than done, my Friend. But I think I'm hearing you.
Thanks.*

LIVE! JUST LIVE!

For eight years—"the comeback years"—I have returned
to that instruction with urgent regularity.

Whenever I begin to see myself as something other than a
man living my life with God, I'm in trouble. Whenever I think
of myself as the pastor, the writer, the Christian leader, or the
community religious symbol, I am on thin ice. I am not any of
those things—not really. I am Bob Girard, a believer in Jesus,
struggling to live the life of a real Christian in the middle of the
very same everyday stuff of which the lives of everyone else in
this community are made. If I walk with my head in those
unrealistic clouds too long, the ice begins to crack under the
weight of ecclesiastical preconceptions, traditional expectations,
ministerial performance, institutional responsibility, and personal inadequacy in the face of the commissions and challenges
of the church. I begin to sink like a millstone into the icy waters
of a kind of spiritual schizophrenia for trying to be bigger than
my own britches!

If I have to carry all that performance baggage, I can't even
see clearly how to take the next human step. I can't see who I
am any more. And the people around me I'm supposed to be
helping can't see me either. All they get is a phony act, a
convoluted caricature of a Christian model—nothing that will
help anybody!

There is no reality in my ministry if it does not flow from
reality in my walk as a man with God. Ecclesiastical showman-
ship doesn't fool anybody; it only confuses them.

I have taken specific steps to keep my focus on living life
and letting ministry flow from that. Before anyone around Lake
Montezuma knew I was a "clergyman," I fulfilled every little

boy's dream by joining the volunteer fire department. It was wonderful! Real friendships were formed before they got all phonied up with stained-glass preconceptions. Before they learned to clean up their language and put on a show for "the preacher," they learned they could trust me as a fellow firefighter and could be themselves with me. The opportunity to be a Christian man among the men has opened up relationships and opportunities to care and serve that I never would have had.

I consciously try not to project a "ministerial image." I go to the store in ragged jeans. Shave only when necessary. Appear in public places with dirty hands and windblown hair. In the village I try to be just what I am. People both in and outside the church have traditional expectations that they project on "the preacher," and I don't always argue about them until I start to feel the iron maiden of that deadly image closing in around me.

When I first joined the Kiwanis Club, I was asked to pray the invocation four weeks in a row. Upon being asked to do so the fifth time I said, "I sure hope I'm not the only guy in this town who knows how to pray!" After that, others were called on too.

I take great delight in driving a school bus as a substitute driver. It gives me a chance to drive those monster vehicles and keeps me in touch with the community's children and the other bus drivers.

Transparency about who I am and what my struggles and joys are is a principle I live by. I'm likely to tell my neighbor when I meet him in the post office about something that's worrying me. I don't always answer the greeting "How are you?" with an automatic "Fine" when I'm hurting. I may tell someone whom I know is not a Christian how I've been praying about something and whether or not I've gotten an answer. I may even confess a problem with temptation or lack of faith. He may as well know that the Christian life doesn't guarantee perfection. And he might just feel a bit more free to talk to me as a friend instead of as "the resident holy man."

"It's not easy bein' green," sings Kermit the Frog in *The Muppet Movie.* I know how he feels. To keep from being treated like something from the Okefenokee Swamp is very difficult once they put "Rev." in front of your name. But in the country or the city or the church, I'll fight for it. To fulfill God's call to "Live, just live!" I must have liberty to move and breathe and work as an authentic human being in a community of human beings.

I look around
   In a world of gifted people
   And wonder, a bit wistfully,
   What is my gift?
   What do I have to give the world?

   The gift of God to each of us
   Is life itself,
   This bubbling, restless force
   That churns inside us,
     That seeks expression and direction
     Like a rushing stream . . .
     Sometimes formed by circumstances
     As a stream is by its banks,
   But never contained by them.
   Moving, changing form,
   Ducking under obstacles, splashing over them . . .

My gift from God?
Life!
     And how twice-gifted I am
     If the stream of my life has been given direction
     By the meaning of Jesus Christ.
                 —*Gordon and Gladis DePree*[2]

Notes

1. Henri Nouwen, "Adam's Peace," *World Vision* (August-September 1988): 5–6.
2. Gordon DePree and Gladis DePree, *The Gift* (Grand Rapids: Zondervan, 1976), 9.

Chapter 7

Behold, the Man!

> Learn the lesson that, if you are to do the work of a
> prophet, what you need is not a scepter but a hoe.
> —*Bernard of Clairvaux*[1]

I HAVE LEARNED to project a strong, manly presence. My
voice is deep and naturally loud. That, combined with a
brusque telephone manner, has caused a few timid women
callers to hang up in tears. Until I discovered what was
happening, I made babies cry just by talking to them. My
handshake, until arthritis took its toll, was firm. In business
meetings I am outspoken and naturally fall into the role of a
leader. At games I am a fierce competitor. I like sports. I like to
work hard enough to sweat. My male hormones are as active as
the next guy's.

But I have been confused about manhood. For most of my
adult life I have felt less than a man. It may have started with
my parents' disappointment that I was not a baby girl and their

obvious favoritism toward my younger sister. Their unintended message: girls are better and more lovable than boys. My father's impatience with me when I worked for him in his grocery ("Can't you do anything right?") left me convinced that I was a mechanical nincompoop with two club hands.

Then the church made me a "clergyman." A professional "saint," whose holy calling set him somehow above the menial. By precept and example, we ministers were taught that our high work is so important that we must not take time for the low work of repairing cars, cleaning, or other dirty duties, but should, wherever possible, recruit or hire someone less gifted to do these things for us so as not to waste time on lesser work than saving souls. The preacher who had to work with his hands for a living was looked down upon as less successful, less professional, or at best, temporarily involved in lesser work until the church could set him free to devote his full time to the ministry.

There were clergymen who continued to work with their hands, some because they had to, and some because they wanted to. They often felt guilty about it. But aside from the guilt, I think they were more healthy men.

In addition to the unwritten law about leaving all physical work to the "less gifted," the expectations of pastoral ministry itself have an emasculating effect. Trying to be what I was expected to be and trying to act like I was expected to act, I lost touch, to a harmful degree, with who and what I really was. Soon it was impossible to think of myself without the "ministerial image." I became an actor (clown?) playing "the pastoral role." In important areas of my self-perception, I stopped being Bob Girard the man, and became "Reverend Girard" or "Pastor" or "Preacher"—the professional Christian holy man who was responsible for the eternal souls of others. Deep inside I knew I was still the human being, the spiritual struggler, the needy, the weak. But that Bob Girard was unacceptable and ugly and needed to remain hidden. From his dark, secret cell he screamed for the light of day, but only a few were permitted to hear his screams. And they didn't sound like the screams of a man, but like a terrified little boy who was still a long way from manhood.

THE GLORY OF GETTING YOUR HANDS DIRTY

An important aspect of the process of coming back from spiritual sickness and failure for me has been a rediscovery of the therapeutic effects of regular work with my hands. I have come to love the feel of good wood, the smell of sawdust, the sound of a hammer driving nails.

Pumping gas

My first taste of manual satisfaction came when we still lived in north Phoenix. I was surprised at how much I enjoyed my part-time job as a filling station attendant, serving the mundane needs of people in their cars. The smell of gas and grease and exhaust. The simple opportunities to help people without having to preach at them. The occasional travel emergency: the paint truck that rolled into the station on fire, on which I emptied the station fire extinguisher. When the fire was out and the truck was saved, I knew I'd done something measurably important.

Valve job

A few months before, in the midst of learning my true identity, I began to doubt my daddy's unthinking injunction about my mechanical ineptitude.

Our '73 Pinto needed a valve job. Jack, a mechanic in our house church, had a garage full of tools. He told me I could do the work in his garage. If I ran into a snag I could call him at his job and he would advise me. All I could lose was a few days time, and a little embarrassment if I had to give up and get a "real mechanic" to finish the job. From the public library I checked out an auto repair manual.

An experienced mechanic could have done in three days

what it took me two weeks to do. But the time was nothing compared to the satisfaction that came with taking that four-cylinder engine apart and putting it back together again, coming home every night with grease beyond my elbows, and straining my brain to work through the mechanical problems involved. Jack and the book led me through it step by step: the gasket work, taking the valves to the machine shop for grinding, setting the timing, turning the bolts to just the right torque.

Two weeks later, I prayed, "Lord, let this thing start." I got behind the wheel, turned the ignition key, and when it started I was so surprised I jumped out of the car and danced all around the garage, shouting, "Praise the Lord! Hallelujah! Whoopee!" until Jack's wife came out of the house to see what all the yelling was about.

I did it, Daddy! You said it couldn't be done, but I did it!

That purring engine, my hopelessly smelly and grease-soaked clothes, and the black goo under my fingernails were my bar mitzvah declaration to the world and to myself, "Today, I am a man!"

What a relief to find out that I was not just a professional puppet dancing on an ecclesiastical string, but a healthy, adult male.

Next Sunday, I was the guest preacher at a local church in Phoenix. I was secretly more excited about the grease still under my fingernails than I was about the content of my sermon.

Firefighting

My family laughs at the way I respond to fire calls. The tone sounds on my volunteer fireman's pager, the adrenalin begins to surge in my veins, the dispatcher's voice gives the location of the fire, and I'm rushing around frantically putting on my "turnouts," dashing out to my pickup truck and throwing gravel as I roar down the hill toward the fire house.

I'm not the community's best fire engineer. The skillful use of all the dials and valves on the pumpers is not natural, my memory for water pressure per foot of hose is faulty, and donning the SCBA air pack sends me into a claustrophobic spasm. But when I'm fighting a fire side by side with my comrades, I feel good about who I am. Coming home from a 2:00 a.m. Saturday night fire call, smelling of smoke, covered with soot and mud, physically exhausted, and having to get up in a couple of hours to get ready to preach Sunday morning, I stand in the shower and enjoy the special sense of rightness, peace, and accomplishment. To be included in the special camaraderie among firefighters is, to me, an important affirmation.

Woodcutting

Living in our country mountain home requires another hand-dirtying task which to me is a special manly pleasure—gathering firewood. Our house is heated with a woodburning fireplace. We get snow and the winter nights are cold, so heat is essential. Usually two or three men will go the forest together, though I have gone alone a few times. Having obtained a Forest Service permit to gather wood, I load my Toyota 4X4 with chainsaw, ax, tools, gas, water, lunch, and Princess, our big, white Samoyed, and head for the high country. I'm in high spirits. I love the woods, the work, and the satisfaction of personally providing my family with its winter warmth. I feel like the man of the house, protector and champion of my family.

These are new feelings for me. Until now, I had given attention to education, professional expertise, public image, religious duties, ecclesiastical protocol, mental growth, and keeping the saints happy—all very important things. But somehow I missed a dimension that is far more important to my spiritual and emotional well-being than I ever realized: the essential satisfaction that comes from useful, physical work.

On a visit to Australia, I learned that Aussies do not normally enter the ministry right out of high school and college, as Americans do. (I was not old enough to vote when I accepted my first pastorate!) After high school, a man takes up a trade or goes into business, works for a few years in the workaday world in which he's going to be ministering, then returns to college or seminary to complete his theological education. After that, he enters the ministry—full grown, experienced in life, in touch with the real world, with some level of spiritual maturity. It makes sense, and it's biblical. Just look at the ages of most Bible people when their work for God began!

I was well into my house-building project when I remembered that Jesus was thirty years a carpenter before his three-plus years as a preacher. My life has been upside down: I tried to be a preacher for thirty years *before* my three-plus years as a carpenter. Until I became a carpenter (even an amateur), I missed some of the vital experiences of a normal human being, experiences that would have made me a happier, better-adjusted person, and may well have made mine a more effective ministry.

GENEALOGY OF THE HOUSE CALLED "EBENEZER"[2]

God kept his promise to help us build a house when we had the least money and building costs were highest. I look around this "saltbox" and see reminder after reminder that *this is the house that the body built*! Dust the place for fingerprints and you'll find overwhelming evidence that this two-story country castle was fabricated by many, many hands that got dirty in Jesus' name.

I never built a house before. I was quite uncertain about my ability to do it. But we knew that if we were ever to have one of our own, we would have to build it ourselves. The Pinto valve job boosted my confidence. The readiness of Christian friends to help in various ways assured us that we would not be without support.

Don Ferguson sold us the lot in Scottsdale at a significant discount and carried the financing. Though we ultimately did not build there, it was an early expression of loving support. Audrey's brother Allen gave us the first two thousand dollars toward our building fund. Bob Jacobs asked a friend to make preliminary drawings from our rough sketches. Bud Hites prepared architectural blueprints and gave them to us as a gift. To aid in calculating the cost, Lauretta Phillips loaned us lists used by the construction company for which she worked. Further help in figuring costs came from Jim Rondeau, a licensed homebuilder.

To this point, we still planned to build the house in Scottsdale.

Our attention was drawn to Lake Montezuma by the lot the people of Our Heritage Church had given us. Jules Klagge made it possible for us to purchase our cliffside site by carrying an interest-free note and conveying the title to us free and clear. When the house was nearly finished and we were living in it, after dribbling $35 per month payments to him for several years so the debt was down to half its original amount, Jules said, with a characteristic twinkle in his eye, "I'm tired of fooling around with these little checks!" So he wrote "Paid in full" across the note and returned it to us.

I decided that if I was going to build this house, I'd need some training. I enrolled in a construction materials class at Maricopa Tech. The teacher was Tom Cadigan, a rough-talking teacher-builder about my age. I told him of my plans and how insecure I felt about building. He suggested I visit some construction sites in the metropolitan area and "if you don't think you can do as good or better, don't do it."

I took his advice, and was shocked at the incidence of crooked foundations and walls and other evidences of careless and inept workmanship. "I think I can do as well as that," I told him at the next class.

Next semester, I enrolled in a class on construction methods. Again, the teacher was Tom Cadigan. We became friends. He loaned me his cement mixer and helped me haul it to Lake Montezuma. A wonderful thing happened: without the artificial barrier of my "Rev." title (which he knew nothing about and I wasn't about to tell him), we were able to like each other as men. On our trip to deliver the cement mixer, I found it easy to enjoy him as a person and to engage him in conversations about spiritual things. He was free to be himself and to be honest, and so was I.

I was shocked to have to admit that Tom's was the first nonevangelical friendship I had made since becoming a pastor more than twenty-seven years before. Until Tom, I wasn't sure I was capable of real friendships beyond the perimeters of professional ministry. My relationships with people outside the church were mostly pastor-and-prospect relationships, not true friendships. All my close friends were Christians. Tom was the first of several man-to-man friendships.

A Christian contractor in the Verde Valley gave us a list of reliable subcontractors. We engaged one of them to install a septic system and dig the footings. Ron, a stranger to us, came out to do the backhoe work. As the big scoop clawed through the thin layer of soil and attacked the limestone just beneath the surface, it became apparent that the place where we wanted to build was a monolith so solid that the foundation would have to be poured into forms mostly above ground level and resting on bedrock.

At one point in the arduous digging, Ron stopped the tractor, pulled off his sweat-soaked baseball cap and declared, "Well, the Lord said to build your house on solid rock. And that's exactly what you're doing!"

When it came time to pour the footings, we were $100 short of enough money to pay for the concrete. A glance at our checking account revealed the awful truth—we had already overdrawn! This forced me to recheck the figures. We were not overdrawn after all—mistakes in subtraction had left us with enough to cover all checks plus the extra $100 we needed for concrete. (Someone said, "Coincidences tend to happen to people who pray.")

Construction of forms for footings was my first major project. I followed as carefully as I could the instructions in the house building manuals I'd purchased. Tom Cadigan came from Phoenix the day the footings were poured. For most of a day we worked together in green "mud" to get a good foundation for the house to rest on. My forms had a tendency to come apart at the corners, requiring several emergency operations to shore them up against the weight of the wet concrete. As the mud dried, we had footings that were fairly level, though they varied in width from sixteen to thirty inches!

"I'll cover 'em up!" I told my professor sheepishly.

Back in Phoenix on Monday night in the construction methods class, Tom told my classmates *all* about the project. Then he looked at me. "Bob," he said, "you flunked forms!"

After the septic system was in and the footings were poured (and the money was gone), we made our decision to move from Phoenix to Lake Montezuma. Neither Audrey nor I had the promise of employment. We just knew it was time.

"Lord, we'll need a place to live while building the house," we prayed.

At the completion of her service at the academy, Audrey withdrew two thousand dollars from her teachers' retirement fund. "Lord," she prayed, "this is all we have to spend on a place to live. Please give us a used mobile home that we can afford, near our lot where we want to park it and with not much furniture so we can use some of our own."

And that is exactly what he provided.

Three of us (four, when son Bobby was home) lived cozily in our 8 x 32 foot house trailer (256 square feet) for two and one-half years.

It wasn't until I went to the county planning and zoning office to apply for a permit to park a mobile home on the lot while building (a zoning variance was required) that we found out that the maximum size allowed was 8 x 32 feet. God had protected us in our ignorance.

Back in Phoenix, Audrey received a letter from Beaver Creek School offering her a half-time job as a "Chapter I" instructor, teaching remedial reading and math.

So we moved, Audrey and Charity and I. "Lock, stock and barrel," as the cliché goes. We furnished the trailer house with our own furniture and stored the rest. That was in June.

We had no money with which to build. And what little

else we had would have to stretch until Audrey's first paycheck in September or until I sold one of my proposed books and, hopefully, received an advance on royalties. No royalties ever came that summer—just two rejection notices. The amount of money we had was divided into small weekly segments, which we doled out to ourselves. Our nearest neighbors had been given a lot of canned goods; they shared with us the things they didn't like. Fortunately our tastes are rather broad!

In midsummer, weary of self-denial, I splurged and brought home a big, four-dollar jar of peanut butter. But before I could get it into the house, I dropped it. The jar shattered, and the peanut butter was lost in the limestone dirt. I wept until there was no point to crying any more. Then we all laughed. The next week we came home from an outing to find a full case—twelve small jars—of Skippy peanut butter, with five twenty-dollar bills stuffed in beside the jars.

In July, contractor-brother Jim Rondeau took me out to his backyard in Phoenix and said, "I don't see how you're going to build that house without a truck to haul materials. I've got this seventy-two Datsun pickup somebody gave me in payment of a bill. It's been rolled. It belonged to a painter who got paint all over it. But it runs good. If you want it, you can have it!"

Sure enough, the truck had plenty of dents. It had no windows except the windshield, and that was cracked in fifty directions. It was a faded blue color with big blotches of white paint that made it look as if it had been camouflaged for flying among the clouds. But it ran. And it had a lumber rack. And even a sun roof. On hot days the driver got hot. And on rainy days he got wet. On cold days he got cold. I loved it and praised God for it every time I got in it to go somewhere.

After toughing it through the summer, we applied for and got two life insurance loans totaling thirteen hundred dollars and resumed building. Sam and Eleanor Wrona, semi-retired barbers, and John Stofko, a retired grocer, laid the concrete block stemwall and taught me how to do it. I laid all the remaining block and brick myself.

A Christian couple and a widow in the church offered

loans at low interest to keep the project going. After accepting the part-time pastorate at Montezuma Chapel, many small gifts were given to help us in the project. A neighbor who claims to be an atheist gave us a hundred dollars. Others gave materials: lumber, concrete block, bricks, nails, tile, doors, half the aluminum windows needed, a sink, medicine cabinets, a water heater, an electric furnace and ductwork, tools, a light fixture, refrigerator, kitchen range and hood, temporary steps, bathroom fixtures from a mansion on Mummy Mountain, and seventeen tons of river rock for the solarium heat storage pit. These were all used or surplus items, but were in usable, working order. We received them with joy!

Many people made tools and equipment available to us.

The former pastor, a woodworking genius, gave us a very special front door he had made personally out of "legend-wood," valued at over three hundred dollars.

A Christian sister, Estelle Cresswell, asked how much we needed for the fireplace-woodstove we planned to install. Surprised, uncertain of the cost, and thinking it was too much to expect as a gift, I stammered and hesitated in my answer. Weary of my equivocating, she asked, "Do you want me to give you a *blank check?*" She was serious.

Waste plumbing I did myself, but the copper supply lines and rough interior plumbing were done by Kip Brees, a local racehorse breeder, and his friend, Rod Hubbard, a licensed plumbing contractor. They did the work on Sunday, during church services, which they did not plan to attend anyway! Three electricians did the wiring—Gene Strain, a Canadian (winter resident) who wired according to Canadian building code and wiring style; Jeff Dykhuis, a young Christian contractor who wired according to the American building code and style; and another brother hired by one of the ladies in the church in a clever strategy to help both him and us, who added his own twists in style.

It was amazing to watch how the Lord would send just the right person with the right expertise at the right time with just the answers or skills we needed. Our neighbor, John Wildman, who had been a surveyor in his younger days, showed up the day I was trying to learn to use a transit for leveling the forms. The very day I was puzzling over how to deal with plastic plumbing, a plumber "dropped by" and answered my questions. Arnold Vandermolen, a professional builder and brother, "just happened" to drive fifty miles for an unannounced visit the day I needed advice about how to solve a leveling problem. A rain shower stopped us just as we started to lay the 2 x 6 decking which is our floor, delaying us long enough to find out we were starting wrong. Two days later, discouraged about the flooring problem, I met Bob Fetveit in a doctor's waiting room in Cottonwood. He had just the ideas needed to solve the flooring problem!

Out of "nowhere" the day I was lugging heavy buckets of concrete up a ten-foot ladder to fill the cores in my block trombe wall, Phinn Walsh, a neighbor, showed up. "I need some exercise," he said, as he helped me finish the job. Noticing the steel I-beam I was about to install as a lintel, he questioned its ability to bear the weight it would be required to support. I returned to my manuals, made a phone call to an expert, and was glad for Phinn's suspicions. The beam wouldn't have borne the weight! Phinn's question averted a catastrophe. I am convinced God sent him, though Phinn would be among the last to think of himself as being sent by God.

Phinn showed up for "exercise" repeatedly. He taught me how to build French doors, and he himself built half the kitchen cabinets. A friendship developed that delighted both of us.

The day I intended to begin raising the roof rafters, seven men—five retired, and all with construction experience (one had built more than 150 houses!)—showed up to help. We literally raised the roof in a single day!

When it was time to panel the cathedral ceiling in the "Great Room," Audrey's Uncle Fred and Aunt Esther (who built four houses of their own in Oregon) arrived—surprise!—on a cross-country trip. They stayed until Fred and I got the job done.

Jim Summerton of Gallery of Woods in Sedona invited me

to use his woodworking shop, equipment, and expertise as a professional cabinet maker and builder of unique furniture to build the spruce and epoxy resin countertop for the kitchen.

Jim Sheltron, an Assembly of God layman involved with me in a men's Bible study group, worked many hours on cabinetry, solarium construction, and other projects. His wife, Ruth, an artist, member of a women's study group I led, did the texturing of all the walls and ceilings.

As the writer of Hebrews said after penning that glorious parade of heroes in the Faith Chapter, "And what more shall I say? for time would fail me to tell of . . . " the Runnels and Poehls with their children, who helped clear the land and set the batter boards; Bob Alms and Carl Conant, who worked cement; Thelma Barnes and Burton Long, who painted; Jim and Sherry Clifford, who pitched in with many hours of work on many projects; Dwight Thompson, who kept my vehicles running and helped erect walls; Vern Poehls, our daughter's husband, who installed the heating and air conditioning; Al Lee, who helped install windows; Bobby Girard, Frank Sheets, Neal Hillyard, Ruth Conant, Enrique, Ron, Pat, Allen, Rod, Rick, Floyd from Duluth, and a couple of complete strangers whose names I didn't get—all of whom left their fingerprints and formed part of a clearly visible fingerprint of God, which we call "Ebenezer—the House on the Rock."

In the process, I learned to do nearly everything involved in building. We built a country home, a modified "salt-box," rustic with lots of warm fir, spruce, and pine, some of it with no finish on the wood. It's ruggedness hides many of my mistakes by making them appear planned. It is filled with French doors (eighteen of them!) inside and out, many of which I built. A fireplace, big bay window, an outdoor atrium garden shower, and a solarium for heating were things we always dreamed of having in a home. Upper bedrooms open onto a deck overlooking the Great Room on one side and an outdoor deck-balcony overlooking the Verde Valley on the other. I personally cut and finished out of 2 x 8 Douglas fir each of the 150 posts that comprise the railings. I'm never so happy as when working with wood. Sweat was my contribution to the family income during the time it took to complete. The work gave me a sense of accomplishment and closure with each completed part of the project. A great feeling of personal gratification continues as we live on in this "house of God's help."

TIME TO BE A DADDY

As a part-time pastor and part-time carpenter, I have found myself free to also be what the full-time ministry never allowed me to be—a full-time parent-husband-servant to my family. (That lack may not have been the fault of the profession, but my fault for not keeping my priorities straight.)

I wasn't there a lot of the time when our older daughter, Christine, needed her daddy. My pursuit of success in the church pushed parenting aside. I was in therapy or just finding my way back from it during my son's last two years of high school. It wasn't a "normal" time, but I did attend his basketball games and was there for him some of the time.

With Charity, our youngest, I was available. She was high on my priority list, above pastoral duties and the call of the church. I was there for transportation, support, and interaction. Her athletic events, plays, music, and school functions were allowed to push church schedules aside. And I've reaped more joys from parenting than when family came second.

Audrey's work progressed from part-time to full-time at the school. Her salary has been the main source of our living. Important manly growth has been demanded by the change in our roles within marriage.

When she first returned to school to finish her teaching degree and then went to work as a teacher, I found myself missing our time together terribly. Where before we had been available to each other all day long, now her days were full of classwork and her nights full of study. I complained to the Lord. And I thought I heard him saying, "Help her find time for you."

"How?" I asked.

And the thought came that I might free some of Audrey's time if I were to cook one evening meal per week for the family.

"Good idea." So I did.

It worked so well I decided I would cook more than one meal per week. I found I enjoyed cooking and got a lot of satisfaction from throwing herbs and spices around the kitchen and following interesting recipes. I was even sometimes quite good at it. And it gave me the sense of closure I needed every day. Before long I was cooking five evening meals per week as well as packing lunches and picking up some other household tasks.

Househusband. Who'd ever have thought the term that stirs such mixed emotions among American males would apply to me? I'm rather proud of the title. To me it says I've finally learned something about servanthood. And fairness. How can it ever be thought to be fair for the working wife to spend as much time on the job as her husband and then come home to do all the housework while that lazy dog vegetates in front of the TV?

The man of God is a servant, like his Lord. Discovery of true manhood comprehends discovery of true servanthood.

THERE WAS A MAN SENT FROM GOD . . .

Through all that I have been describing, the call to serve God and the church in ministry has become more intense and genuine than it ever seemed before. Working with my hands and learning to be a man among men, a father to my children, and a servant to my wife have not dulled my concern for the gospel or the *ecclesia* in the slightest. If anything, they have cleansed and sharpened it. I am as deeply connected and committed to the body of Christ as ever. Even though by choice I receive only "part-time" pastoral support, I see my whole life as ministry. I see this little congregation as my family. It's not a "part-time" relationship at all. I cannot see my life apart from them.

The carpenter has been sent back out to preach. Hopefully his message is more healthy and complete.

> He worked the wood and drove
> the pegs methodically.
>
> The shavings from the adze
> piled high upon the floor.
>
> "Earthmaker, full of mercy,"
> he said, when evening had
> come, "I am a tradesman!"
>
> "No," said the silent air,
> "not a tradesman—a troubadour instead!"
>
> "A tradesman!" he said firmly
> as he smashed his mallet on the vise.
>
> "A troubadour!" the silence
> thundered back.
>
> —*Calvin Miller*, The Singer[3]

Notes

1. Richard J. Foster, *Celebration of Discipline* (San Francisco: Harper & Row, 1978), 110.
2. The biblical genealogies with all their unfamiliar names and "begats" are not the most exciting reading, but they are essential to the story. Some may find this genealogy dry in spots. But to Audrey and me, nothing illustrates the significance of "Ebenezer" (Rock of the Lord's Help), or the support of the body like the way our house became a reality.
3. Calvin Miller, *The Singer* (Downers Grove, Ill.: InterVarsity Press, 1975).

Chapter 8

The Pathway to Success

> There is no defeat unless one loses God—then all is
> defeat though it be housed in castles and buried in
> fortunes.   —*Frank Laubach*

IN THE AGONY of my defeats, trying to explain myself to
myself, I turned to the Word. I desperately wanted to believe
what my spirit insisted—that God still accepted me in spite of
the awesomeness of my ineffectiveness. I had to know how
God actually was evaluating me in the light of the failures in my
ministry, my sanity, and my relationships. God's view of
success and failure would surely be found in the Bible.

My research uncovered a significant fact: neither testament
uses a word that exactly coincides with "success" or "failure"
as we understand the terms. That, I discovered, is because
God's view of success and failure is quite different from ours.

In Western culture our judgment of a man or his work as
success or failure usually hangs on such things as wealth and

security, public acceptance and notoriety, power and influence, physical beauty and talent, visible accomplishment, or the lack of these things. Equipped with these criteria, the world may look at that person and pronounce him and his work a flop, while God pronounces him a success, and the person himself knows he's spiritually rich.

THE DICTIONARY DEFINITIONS
Webster's New Universal Unabridged Dictionary, 1983

suc-cess' n. [OFr. *succes*; L. *successus*, result, event, fr. *succedere*, to succeed]
   1. result, outcome [*Obs.*]
   2. a favorable or satisfactory outcome or result
   3. the gaining of wealth, fame, rank, etc.
   4. a successful person or thing
Syn.—achievement, luck, consummation, prosperity, victory
fail'-ure n. **1.** a falling short; deficiency; cessation of supply, or total defect; as, the failure of springs or streams; failure of rain; failure of crops
   2. omission or neglect; a not doing; as failure to obey rules
   3. decay; a weakening; a dying away; as the failure of memory or of sight
   4. a becoming insolvent or bankrupt; as, there were many failures that year
   5. a not succeeding in doing or becoming
   6. a person or thing that does not succeed; as, she was an utter failure as an actress
   7. in education **a** : a failing to pass **b** : a grade or mark (usually F) indicating a failing to pass
   8. a failing; a slight fault [*Obs.*]

The world's success mentality has a firm grip on the thinking of the church and its ecclesiastical structures. Without a thought that there might be another way to approach the matter, or that there may be important factors that are being overlooked, churchmen pronounce a congregation, a pastor, a mission, a Christian enterprise, or themselves successful and "blessed of God," or failing, on the basis of the same worldly criteria. But such measurements may not be relevant to success as God gauges it. The biblical standards cut much deeper into the soul and spirit of a man or a work.

THE SUCCESS-BLESSING

Genuine success comes to men and women only in the context of relationship with God.

In Old Testament Hebrew the word "bless" is *barak*. The fact that it appears 415 times in the Old Testament[1] shows it to be an important concern of God's people. *To bless means "to endue with power for success, prosperity, fecundity, longevity, etc."*[2]

The Amplified Bible interprets it:

Blessed—happy, fortunate, prosperous and enviable—is the man who . . . (Ps. 1:1).

The Psalms spell out the Old Testament formula for success.

The first psalm is called *The Preface Psalm,*[3] because it seems to be the text from which the Psalms unfold as a wonderful, divine sermon in which God defines success and failure. Every man wants to succeed. Every man wants to avoid failure. So God gives Israel a hymnbook full of songs that put his concept of prosperity into their mouths. If their hearts are open while they sing, they will sing their way to understanding precisely what success is and how to obtain it.

God is the source of all success-blessing—the only source of true success. "Surely, O LORD, you bless the righteous," sings Psalm 5:12. God, through the covenants, committed himself to make Israel successful. "See," God said in Deuteronomy 11:26–28, "I am setting before you today a blessing and a curse—blessing [success] if you obey . . . the curse [failure][4] if you disobey the commands of the LORD . . . by following other gods." All through the Old Testament, success is promised on these terms.

The genuinely successful person is described in the Psalms

(and the rest of the Old Testament) as a person who is living by faith in vital personal relationship with God and in obedience to the Word of God. That is the only context in which God is free to give his richest, most abundant life to a person.

THE FAILURE-CURSE

To fail means to go from fullness to emptiness, from large-souledness to small-souledness, from spiritual prosperity to poverty.

The Hebrew Old Testament has no word that can be directly translated "failure." When English translators use the word "fail" they are interpreting one of several Hebrew terms that have meanings like "to be at an end, to be cut off, to pass over, to sink or relax, to be at a distance, or to stumble."[5] However, speaking in Deuteronomy 11:26–28, God uses the word "curse" to signify the opposite of "blessing" (success). "Curse" is the Hebrew noun *qalalah*. Young interprets it as "a reviling, a thing lightly esteemed."[6] Larry Richards says it "emphasizes the loss or absence of the state of blessing." The verb *qalal* indicates "the blessing withdrawn."[7]

God's contract with Israel left no doubt as to how to succeed or fail. Obedience to the commandments of the Lord is the secret of success, and disobedience to the commandments of the Lord is the pathway to withdrawal of God's blessing, reduced position, reduced power, reduced wealth, reduced honor, and a broken relationship with God—which is the substance of failure.[8]

THE NATURE OF SUCCESS

The changed person, not his measurable accomplishments, is the success for which God is looking.

In Matthew 5, Jesus opens his Sermon on the Mount with the same word with which David begins Psalm 1—"Blessed." Chances are Jesus used the same Hebrew word, *barak*. The Greek word is *makarios*. Squeezing out all the richness of meaning embodied in the biblical usage, the Amplified version defines it:

> Blessed—happy, to be envied, and spiritually prosperous [that is, with life-joy and satisfaction in God's favor and salvation, regardless of their outward conditions] (Matt. 5:3).
>
> . . . enviably happy, [with a happiness produced by experience of God's favor and especially conditioned by the revelation of His matchless grace] (v. 4).
>
> . . . blithesome, joyous (v. 5).
>
> . . . enviably fortunate (v. 8).

In a word, successful!

Jesus gives the ancient concept a twist: the emphasis is on experiencing inner spiritual riches amid external poverty and trial. In the midst of even the most difficult of circumstances, God's blessing makes us prosperous and fortunate. Others may look and see poverty, mourning, hunger, sacrifice, and persecution, but we know we are successful, wealthy, and favored.

Nothing puts the lie to the modern Christian success cult like the statements of kingdom principle we call the Beatitudes. They represent a perspective on personal prosperity that turns today's success mentality on its head. They are a slap in the face to the value systems of multiplied Christians and their churches.

> Successful are the poor in spirit,
>   for theirs is the kingdom of heaven.
> Successful are those who mourn,
>   for they will be comforted.
> Successful are the meek,
>   for they will inherit the earth.
> Successful are those who hunger and thirst for
>   righteousness,
>   for they will be filled.
> Successful are the merciful,
>   for they will be shown mercy.
> Successful are the pure in heart,
>   for they will see God.

Successful are the peacemakers,
for they will be called sons of God.
Successful are those who are persecuted because of
righteousness
for theirs is the kingdom of heaven.
Successful are you when people insult you, persecute you
and falsely say all kinds of evil against you because of
me. Rejoice and be glad, because great is your reward
in heaven, for in the same way they persecuted the
prophets who were before you (Matt. 5:3–12).

It is immediately clear that Jesus is not giving us the standard formula for worldly success. He turns everything upside down. He redefines success, prosperity, and happiness. They have nothing to do with worldly wealth, power, or honor. Such things may actually undermine true success. True success is the inner riches of character conformed to God's own.

Authentic Christian success is in the riches of—

Vulnerability (v. 3). Success is when a person freely and openly acknowledges that there is a gap between the spiritual possibilities and spiritual realities of his life, and that he is in himself utterly without the resources needed to deal with the gaps.

Brokenness (v. 4). Success is when a person experiences true brokenness and sorrow over his own sins and the sickness of the world. His soul is getting rich when he allows his heart to be broken by what breaks the heart of God.[9]

Gentleness (v. 5). When a person perceives and accepts the truth that he owns nothing but God, he is becoming truly prosperous. The genuinely successful people are those who claim nothing[10] and demand nothing; who, ceasing from rebellion, place themselves under the reins of the Master,[11] are thoroughly teachable and continually seek to relinquish themselves totally to God. This kind of personal richness becomes visible as gentleness of style.

Intensity (v. 6). Success is a person seeking godliness as though his life depends on it. He wants God's righteousness and seeks God's mind above all other pursuits—as a starving man wants food and a man dying of thirst craves water.[12]

Compassion (v. 7). The lives of genuinely successful people are marked by the "inefficiency" of deeply felt concern for persons and their healing. They care enough to choose to do the costly, time-consuming work of getting inside the lives of others to experience what they experience, feel what they feel, know what they know,[13] so that help can meet real, not imaginary, needs.

Single-mindedness (v. 8). Successful people are cleansed people whose hearts are undefiled by their own evil and unencumbered by self-generated virtues.[14] They have surrendered their hearts completely to Jesus so that he alone may reign in them.

Propitiation (v. 9). To be successful is to be a reconciler, bringing alienated persons together into a community of love. Fulfillment is found in a definite, positive, active, initiating involvement in the troubles and conflicts of people, not in detachment and distance or escape from them.[15]

Rejection by the world (vv. 10–12). To succeed is to be crucified.[16] Those rich in his prosperity are those who are ready to follow Jesus to the loss of all things. Their lifestyle, an espousal of the values of Christ, is so radically contradictory to the world's priorities and ways, so radiant a prophetic condemnation of cultural practices and values, that it brings them into rejection and trouble.

Jesus describes the nature of success in terms of the personal attitudes and qualities that inevitably develop when the blessing of God is present.

FAILURE'S BOTTOM LINE

True failure is to fail to be recognized as belonging to Christ.

A definitive New Testament statement on failure comes near the end of the Sermon on the Mount, in Matthew 7:

Not everyone who says to me, "Lord, Lord," will enter the kingdom of heaven, but only he who does the will of my Father who is in heaven. Many will say to me on that day, "Lord, Lord, did we not prophesy in your name, and in your name drive out demons and perform many miracles?" Then I will tell them plainly, "I never knew you. Away from me, you evildoers!" (Matt. 7:21–23).

Jesus does not discuss whether the miracles are real. Sometimes miracles are reported where none have occurred. And God can work real miracles around even very wicked men for sovereign reasons of his own, or for the sake of the faith of simple, needy people. The pagan soothsayer Balaam pronounced God's true message, even though he was carnally motivated and had no intention of serving God (Num. 22–25). The high priest Caiaphas prophesied, even while plotting to kill him, that Jesus would give his life for the nation and the world (John 11:49–52).

People are known to have been brought to authentic faith in Christ under the preaching of corrupt evangelists. Prophecy, miracles, and driving out demons are not proofs of spiritual success. The powerful spiritual leader who claims to be accomplishing great things in Christ's name, but who refuses to allow the will of God to shape his personal life and character is actually a stranger to Christ. That alienation is what produces the evil spiritual fruit by which false prophets are recognized (Matt. 7:15–20). Not to be recognized by Christ as one of his is to fail!

A MATTER OF LIFE AND DEATH

To fail is to exist in a state of separation from God—and then to go out into eternity without him.

The primary concern in the Bible's discussion of success and failure (blessing and cursing) is not self-esteem, personal fulfillment, or evaluation of an individual's "gross personal product." Biblical success and failure have deep spiritual and eternal consequences. The real issue is stated by God in Deuteronomy 30:19:

> This day I call heaven and earth as witnesses against you that I have set before you *life and death,* blessings and curses. Now choose *life,* so that you and your children may *live* and that you may love the LORD your God, listen to his voice, and hold fast to him. For the LORD is your *life* (italics added).

To fail, in biblical terms, is not merely to live a poverty-stricken, small-souled life in which there is no true personal fulfillment or sense of accomplishment. To fail (to try to live without God) is to die.

SUCCESS AND MATERIAL PROSPERITY

The Bible encourages the expectation that if things are right between people and God, material abundance will follow.

"Whatever he [the blessed man] does prospers," promises Psalm 1:3. Primarily this means spiritual prosperity, the abundance that comes to the soul who lives with God.

However, the Old Testament assumes that God's blessing brings with it material prosperity too. There are many specific promises that state this truth. For example:

> Observe the commands of the LORD your God, walking in his ways and revering him. For the LORD your God is bringing you into a good land—a land with streams and pools of water, with springs flowing in the valleys and hills; a land with wheat and barley, vines and fig trees, pomegranates, olive oil and honey; a land where bread will not be scarce and you will lack nothing; a land where the rocks are iron and you can dig copper out of the hills. When you have eaten and are satisfied, praise the LORD your God for the good land he has given you (Deut. 8:6–10).

The promise is immediately followed by a warning. If, after God has made them rich in houses, herds, flocks, silver, and gold "and all you have is multiplied," they become proud and think they have won prosperity by their own strength and hard work, and if they forget the Lord and give allegiance to other gods, they will be destroyed! This same destiny awaits any nation that refuses to obey the Lord God (Deut. 8:12–20).

The link between material prosperity and relationship with God is unmistakable. But sometimes other issues are at stake.

GOOD GUYS ONLY SEEM TO FINISH LAST

The biblical portrait of spiritual success is often a picture of people surviving amid harassment, trouble, poverty, disaster, and famine.

Merely amassing material wealth and the power that goes with it is not success. Many wealthy, powerful people are in rebellion against God. God declares them of slight value (cursed). With Psalm 37, David composed a song against evil men who "succeed in their ways, when they carry out their wicked schemes" (v. 7). Clearly, the plutocracy of which David sings did not gain its power because of God's promises, but climbed to power and wealth on the backs of the oppressed. They possess wealth while the righteous have little (v. 16). They hold the power (v. 17). They flourish "like a green tree in its native soil" (v. 35). But they have no future (vv. 9–10, 15, 17, 38). They will be brought down in full view of the righteous poor whom they have oppressed (v. 34).

The secret of the resilience of the righteous is that they trust God (v. 3). He is the delight of their lives (v. 4), their way is committed to him (v. 5), and they are waiting for his justice (v. 6). They are promised a home (v. 3), security (vv. 3, 27), their heart's desire (v. 4), justice (v. 6), peace (v. 11), protection (vv. 14–15, 28), support (vv 17, 24), plenty to eat (vv. 19, 25), enough to share with others (vv. 21, 26), blessing/success (v. 22), confidence (v. 23), God's love (v. 28), deliverance (v. 33), a future (v. 37), salvation (v. 39), a refuge from the wicked (vv. 39–40), the Lord's help (v. 40). A wonderful inventory of success with God in the midst of very difficult circumstances.

The promise of Psalm 37 is more spiritual abundance than

material prosperity. We're led to expect that our basic necessities will be supplied, but not that trusting God will bring us into a cushy life.

THE IMMINENT FAILURE OF WORLDLY SUCCESS

Those who build their own security at the expense of others are headed nowhere and will ultimately possess nothing.

The book of Habakkuk is filled with warnings against selfish security. In chapter 1, the prophet complains to God about the injustice that is rampant in Judah in his day. In his opinion, God has tolerated violence and perversion of justice too long! The law is powerless to bring the wealthy and powerful to account (vv. 2–4).

God's response is, "I am raising up the Babylonians" (v. 6).

God is God, Habakkuk acknowledges. He can bring needed judgment through the godless Babylonians if he wishes (v. 12). But those pagan instruments of justice, who seem to be experiencing such success, are themselves treacherous and wicked men who devour not only the damnable oppressors who deserve punishment but the righteous along with them. Something doesn't seem quite right about that. How can a holy God let the guilty Babylonians get away with their cruelty? (vv. 13–17).

The Lord's answer is that even while they seem to be succeeding, the judgment of the Babylonians has already begun. Their conquests, their ill-gotten accumulation of the spoils of the world, mask the negative spiritual dynamics at work in their lives.

With all their apparent prosperity, they are souls never satisfied, never at rest, blinded by the wine with which they try to dull the inner ache (Hab. 2:4–5). As fast as they gather their wealth, they collect enemies who hate them and dedicate themselves to their destruction (vv. 6–8). Safety eludes them, even though they surround themselves with every security device (vv. 9–11). They are destined for emptiness and poverty (vv. 12–14). They have stripped others naked; they will stand exposed in shame before the world (vv. 15–17). Everything they have built their lives on will prove useless in the pursuit of life and guidance (vv. 18–19).[10] They will be left speechless in the presence of the Lord—no defense, no excuses, nothing to give as evidence of true accomplishment (v. 20).

People who are impressed with human power and glory cannot help but be impressed with that mighty Babylonian war machine and the glory of Nebuchadnezzar's empire. But the prophecies of Habakkuk strip the glamour away and show the hidden failure behind it all. Babylonian successes only slightly veiled the hidden curse eating away at sick, shriveled Babylonian souls.

WHERE IS PROSPERITY WHEN YOU'VE LOST EVERYTHING?

Success and blessing do not depend upon material prosperity; they are found in the joy of knowing God as Savior.

When we know the rest of the story of Habakkuk and his people, we know that the righteous remnant of Judah was carried off into captivity along with those who deserved God's wrath. Everything they owned was taken from them. How, in this scenario, does God keep his promises of blessing/success to his true people?

Habakkuk 3 is a prophetic poem set to music. Habakkuk sings in awe of God and his mighty deeds. He is all-powerful and has at his disposal all the forces of heaven and earth. "Suddenly Habakkuk is shown the overwhelming waters of judgment, rushing like some Genesis cataclysm . . . to burst over the prophet and his people."[17] He trembles with fear; his knees buckle (vv. 15–16). He knows he too will taste the bitter disaster that is coming on the whole nation. True believers will not escape. Where will those who trust God find happiness and see the prosperity God promises when starvation, deprivation, and defeat are the orders of the day?

Habakkuk knows:

> Though the fig tree does not bud
>   and there are no grapes on the vines,
> though the olive crop fails
>   and the fields produce no food,
> though there are no sheep in the pen
>   and no cattle in the stalls,
> yet will I rejoice *in the* LORD,
>   I will be joyful in God my Savior,
> The Sovereign LORD is my strength;
>   he makes my feet like the feet of a deer,
> he enables me to go on the heights.
>
> (Hab. 3:17–19)

Success and blessing did not always mean material prosperity even for Old Testament saints, who had been taught the connection between God's blessing and material abundance.

WE SHARE SOCIETY'S FAILURE

A person may, at one and the same time, be experiencing success with God and the external consequences of society's failure.

Like Habakkuk, we are citizens of the heavenly kingdom, living in responsive relationship to God. At the same time we live in this judgment-bound world and often suffer along with our godless neighbors. God is our refuge and strength. Every believer has experienced the miraculous protection of the Lord. But God does not build a bubble around his people to keep all the world's disasters away.

Joshua illustrates still another aspect of this.

SUCCESS, FAILURE, AND SPIRITUAL KIN

A person may experience success (the personal blessing of God) and at the same time, with his spiritual brothers and sisters, be experiencing failure (withdrawal of the blessing from the body).

"Get ready to cross the Jordan River," God said to Joshua (Josh. 1). "I am about to give Israel the land I've been promising them. You'll have it all—every place you step on—from here to the Great Sea."

God made his promise very personal. "As long as you live, Joshua, no one will be able to stand up against you and win! I'm with you as I was with Moses. I will never leave you or forsake you.

"Here's the secret of your success: Be strong and courageous. Be careful to obey all my instructions. Don't deviate from full obedience to my law. Don't stop muttering my words to yourself. Over and over, day and night, remind yourself of my instructions so that you fully obey all that I've said. Remember my promise to be with you. Don't permit fear or discouragement to alter your trust in me or your responsiveness to me. Then you will be prosperous and successful!" (Josh. 1).

Joshua's response was to believe God. Immediately he sent messengers to tell the people to get ready to march in three days.

The pageant of success and victory began. The knees that buckled with fear were the enemies'. Joshua and Israel witnessed miracles. The mighty Jordan River stood aside to let them pass. Great cities fell before their awestruck eyes. They were instruments of God's judgment on cultures so corrupt they could only be utterly destroyed. They were so obedient, so God-conscious, so holy, so victorious . . . until Ai.

At the tiny town of Ai, the army of God was set to rout (Josh. 7). Thirty-six men were killed. A single soldier had disobeyed orders and taken into his tent some of the forbidden spoil of Jericho. Thus the whole nation was brought to its knees.

Joshua fell down before the Ark of the Covenant and poured out his bitterness to the Lord. Where were all the promises of God now? Fear and discouragement were on his lips as he contemplated the annihilation of the nation.

If success is a healthy relationship with God, even at this

dark moment of failure, Joshua himself was a success. He poured out his heart to God, and found God listening. When God spoke, Joshua obeyed. His heart was set on God. That's the essence of true success.

Nonetheless, his work was coming down around his ears. That such a duality can exist in the life of a man like Joshua provides a very important insight. For most people of God, success and failure are experienced on two distinct levels, the personal and the corporate.

In God's design, his people are so inseparably bound to one another that if one suffers all suffer. If one is blessed, all are blessed (1 Cor. 12:26). The failure of one belongs to all. The failure of the nation or body belongs to each one.

A man may, at the same time, know the joy of personal acceptance by God and the sting of failure in the spiritual family. That is why it is a mistake to credit the success or failure of a church to a single leader. Conversely, it can also be dangerous for a person to think that he is a spiritual success simply because he is part of a successful work. Personal spiritual success is based on personal spiritual choices.

Joshua could control the shape of his own relationship with God. But he could neither take credit for the blessing of God on the others, nor accept all the blame for the curse. He was one part of the whole. His experience of blessing or cursing was inseparably tied to the spiritual choices of his brothers and sisters.

SUCCESS IN THE CHURCH

Faithfulness to the person and instructions of the Lord Jesus is the first measure of church success, not size and power.

In a day of supermarkets, superconductors, Super Bowls, superstars, and supercities, "superchurches" would have to follow. And there are some colossal ones in the world. Paul Yonggi Cho's congregation in Seoul, Korea, grows so fast that any report of its size is out of date before it can published.

Churches of ten thousand are not common, but everybody knows of several.

Even so, the average size for evangelical congregations worldwide is still under one hundred. Some of the "super-churches" are wonderfully healthy. Some are not. Many small churches are ingrown and lifeless. Some are vibrant and dynamic with spiritual energy. The big churches insist that their numerical growth is a sign of spiritual liveliness. But often other factors are involved, like the public's natural attraction to "superstars," the desire of many to be "where the crowds are," the relationally undemanding character of the large church, the desire of many to escape binding commitments, and population concentrations. The little churches struggle with guilt by comparison, even though they may be doing exactly what they are called to do—and doing some things *better* than the superchurches are.

In the book of Acts, the numerical growth of the church among the Jews in the first two or three decades after Pentecost was phenomenal (Acts 2:41; 4:4; 6:7; 21:20). Jewish historian Josephus wrote that one-third of the Jews of his day (A.D. 37–95) had embraced Christianity. In places like Ephesus and Rome, the early Christians had great numerical success. Eventually the Christians even gained the upper hand in the political structures of Rome and thereby became the ruling class.

Numbers simply cannot tell the whole story. Statistics and influence are not wholly reliable barometers of church success. The church at Philadelphia was given high marks by the risen Christ as he moved among the seven churches (Rev. 2–3), even though he admitted they were a congregation of "little strength" (3:8). Their success was that they "have kept my word and have not denied my name." No one is ever commended because he has built a bigger church or seen more converts through his ministry. Those things are matters of God's sovereign working.

Statistics had a place in the Acts record, but spiritual success was also measured in terms of their corporate experience of unity (4:32), imprudent sharing with one another (4:32, 34–35), power to witness regardless of the response (4:33), being recognized as having been with Jesus (4:13), suffering for Jesus' name's sake (5:41), concern for widows (6:1–6), one martyr dying for his faith while loving his executioners (7:59–60), going 150 miles (round trip) to baptize one Ethiopian (8:26–38), one Pharisee converted (9:4–19), risking one's reputation to evangelize the household of a foreigner (10:34–48), and faithfulness in the face of opposition. The reverses were cause for as much joy as the victories.

SUCCESS AND THE CROSS

Jesus promises a personal cross for each disciple, and a corporate cross for each church, where the deeds of the flesh can die and the qualities of the character of Christ himself can emerge. This is true success.

The success Jesus had promised his followers is like his own. A cross is its price tag, resurrection its ultimate promise, life its greatest gift, holiness its sweetest product. Human weakness, surrender, rejection, slander, and suffering are its path, God's glory its destiny. "The servant is not greater than his Lord," Jesus said. And then he went on to win it all . . . at the cross!

Christians who think God exists to give them ease and riches bother me. They promise more than the Bible does. Scriptural promises of prosperity and success must be defined by Scripture itself, not by the faulty logic and wishful thinking of half-blind people who have gotten their theology confused with carnal dreams of affluence. Actually they promise *less* than Jesus does. He promises success-blessing by means of the cross.

Success seemed an on-again-off-again experience for Paul and Barnabas. Sometimes whole communities became followers of Jesus Christ. Sometimes the resistance to their message was impenetrable. Whether they were preaching to the whole city as at Pisidian Antioch (Acts 13:44) or picking themselves up from the bloody stone pile at Lystra (14:19–20), they were fulfilling their mission and experiencing the prosperity of the Lord.

From the viewpoint of his peers, Paul was a greater success when his name was still Saul and he had succeeded in destroying the church at Jerusalem. After Jesus confronted him on the Damascus Road, Paul was told that he was God's "chosen instrument to carry my name before the Gentiles and their kings and before the people of Israel" and that the successful completion of that purpose would involve "much" suffering (Acts 9:15–16).

Thereafter, when Paul stood before kings sharing the gospel, that was success, fulfillment, prosperity and blessedness—chains and all! In 2 Corinthians 11, he penned a painful accounting of all he had suffered for Christ's name, including his ongoing "concern for all the churches" and his tendency to suffer with every Christian's weakness and to burn with every Christian's failure (vv. 28–29). He called it an inventory of "weaknesses." Actually, it is the story of fulfillment and blessing. All those struggles were part of exactly what he had been sent to do.

SUCCESS AND COMPROMISE

The church or work that prospers because it gives people what they want instead of what they need is not succeeding. It is failing miserably, even though numbers may increase.

We are often called upon by the spirit of God to do and say things that actually hinder statistical progress. Case in point: the events of John 6.

The chapter begins with one of Jesus' most wonderful miracles. "A great crowd of people" (the number given is "five thousand *men*," evidently not counting women and children who might have swelled the number to twice that figure) was fed till they were full with "five small barley loaves and two small fish" (a boy's lunch). Twelve baskets of leftovers were gathered after the meal. A grateful crowd of mostly poor people living hand-to-hand were ready to crown him king of Israel (v. 15). "This is God's promised prophet!" they said.

With the kingdom lying at his feet, the thousands of adoring followers calling for him to reign over them, Jesus appeared to have won the hearts of the nation. But something about this apparent success disturbed him deeply. So he disappeared into the hills to pray.

The next day, when the crowd caught up with him on the other side of the lake, he confronted them with the worldliness of their motives: "You are looking for me, not because you saw proof that God has sent me, but because you ate the barley bread and filled your stomachs!" (v. 26). They were willing to work for his coronation because they thought he could make their lives easier. What they must do instead is to hunger and thirst for *him*, eat his flesh and drink his blood spiritually, and live their lives in him. Eternal, spiritual life could only come through feeding their spirits on the person Jesus (v. 47–58).

It was not the message they wanted to hear. They turned away by the thousands. Jesus turned and saw a mere dozen men who had not gone away, and he asked, "You do not want to leave too, do you?" (v. 67).

Peter replied for the Twelve: "Lord, to whom shall we go? You have the words of eternal life. We believe and know that you are the Holy One of God."

If that had been annual report time, the district board of administration might have been called into urgent session to consider how to recoup the terrible losses the church had experienced under Pastor Jesus. When the numbers began to come back, and the crowd who witnessed his resurrection was tallied at "five hundred brethren" (1 Cor. 15:6), it would provide a little comfort. But some people would always feel nostalgic about the "glory days" before Jesus got radical and attendance hit in excess of five thousand. He could have kept the crowds and gained the crown with a little discreet compromise. Common sense would have softened what he knew would be a message impossible for some to receive. But had he held back the unvarnished truth that they must "eat his flesh and drink his blood" in order to live, who could have been saved?

The temptation to avoid certain aspects of biblical truth is all but irresistible for many of us. We care about "our" people. We look into their faces, aware of their prejudices, blind spots, and motivations. If we press every biblical issue, many will be offended and lost to us, or worse, lost to the gospel. If we can keep them coming back, we reason, we can lead more of them to Christ and help them to grow. So in the interest of church growth, we avoid speaking out on some issues Jesus would certainly have addressed.

When he goes to church, the average churchgoer is likely to hear something that supports his worldly lifestyle and attitudes, rather than upsetting and renewing them.

Jesus wouldn't do that.

Jesus intends to be Lord. Every true disciple is learning to bow to his demands, even though they call for difficult personal changes. Merely gathering people together who have "made a decision for Christ" is not the fulfillment of the Great Commission. The commission also includes "teaching them to observe *everything* that I [Jesus] have commanded" (Matt. 28:20). If the only way to keep the church together is to muzzle Jesus, statistical success may be an indication that something is radically wrong.

SUCCESS AND WORKS OF POWER

Our sense of abundance in life comes not through focus on accomplishments or power, but through knowing we are recognized by Christ as one of his.

Even spiritual giftedness and miraculous accomplishments do not signal true success. In Luke 10, Jesus sent out seventy-two of his disciples into the cities of Israel. He gave them authority over diseases and demons (vv. 9, 19). On their return they were ecstatic. "Lord, even the demons submit to us in your name!" Ordinary disciples had become God's men of faith and power! They felt invincible.

Jesus set the record straight in his reply: "I superintended the fall of Satan. It's by *my* authority you are able to trample him under your feet. In *me* you are invincible. However, your joy should not be based on seeing miracles. You should be rejoicing because God has accepted you [your names are written in heaven]" (vv. 17–20, paraphrased).

Authentic personal success and satisfaction do not have to do with miracles or crowds. These things are the works of God and are in his hands. His working in his people varies greatly from one to another (Matt. 13:23; 1 Cor. 12:4–6). Focus on "accomplishments" or "power" leads to comparison, jealousy and pride. The working is *God's*. To God be the glory. Success for us centers in our relationship with God. It has nothing to do with the expectations of church hierarchies, ecclesiastical professionalism, institutional goals, or public image. It does not hinge on whether the world or one's peers considers the work a success. It does not even have to do with the comparative presence or absence of power. Statistics alone are never an adequate way to measure true blessedness-success. Real success has everything to do with what a man or woman is and how fully God is being formed in him or her.

TESTING THE WORKER AND HIS WORK

A person's work is successful if the test of time and the judgment of God reveal it to be a work of faith, a work of the Holy Spirit, and a work of love.

The word *adokimos* is translated "to fail" in 2 Corinthians 13:5–7. It means "to be disqualified as not standing the test, and thus to fail."[18] If Christ is in you, Paul says, you do not fail the test. The proof of success (Christ in you) is that you do what is right and not what is wrong. That is success.

In 1 Corinthians 3, the apostle gives further perspectives on the matter of testing workers and their work.

First, *testing is not comparison* (vv. 1–4). Comparing Christian workers (an inevitable result of the world's success mentality) leads to jealousy, quarreling, divisiveness, and perpetual spiritual infancy. Immature Christians like to think that they are better than others if they line up behind the "better" (more successful) leader or the "better" (more successful) church. "More successful," as the flesh measures, is not necessarily better at all. But baby Christians like to think so. And they'll never grow up as long as they insist on this carnal game of one-upmanship.

If it is spiritually childish to compare leaders with each other, it is equally infantile to compare one's own work with that of others. It indicates an incomplete understanding of the nature of Christian work and one's place in it.

Second, *God, not the worker, produces the increase in the work* (vv. 5–10). The worker is not an independent contractor, he is merely a servant through whom the Lord works. There is no growth, no success, nobody comes to Christ, apart from the working of God. There is no such thing as Paul's work or Apollos' work or Peter's work or my work—there is only God's work.

Third, *co-working with God has its rewards* (vv. 8, 14). Someone suggested that the reward for working with God is to gain a crown we can throw down in worship at his feet (2 Tim. 4:8; Rev. 4:10–11).

Both Jesus and Paul provide glimpses into the nature of the Christian's reward for work. In 1 Corinthians 4, Paul urges Christians not to judge workers (themselves or each other) before "the appointed time." "Wait till the Lord comes," he says. "At that time each will receive his praise from God" according to the *motives* of his heart (v. 5). In the talent parable Jesus puts unforgettable words into the mouth of the Christ-figure (the king):

> Well done, good and faithful servant! . . . Come and share your master's happiness! (Matt. 25:23).

If my work brings happiness to my King, that will be a great reward.

Fourth, *a person's work is judged by its quality* (1 Cor. 3:10–12). It is not human excellence that counts. There is something to be said for wholehearted commitment to Christ, which gives him the very best of one's talents and energy. But what makes a work "gold, silver, costly stones" (which survive the fire) instead of "wood, hay or straw" (which will likely be wiped out in the fire, v. 12) is not human excellence.

When Paul urges the Philippians to "work out your salvation with fear and trembling," he immediately gives them the secret of the work: "for it is God who works in you to will and to act according to his good purpose" (Phil. 2:12–13). Work that fulfills God's purposes and stands the fiery test is work *God does in us*. Two things open the way for work of this caliber: faith and love.

> The only thing that counts is faith expressing itself through love (Gal. 5:6).

The energy for "gold-silver-precious-stones quality" work is inside the Christian in the person of the Holy Spirit. His power is released through faith, which means yielding, giving place to the Spirit of God to do his work in both oneself and the people who are the focus of the work. Precious and indestructible work is produced in a context of dependence on him, not on ourselves.

The only motivation that can give rise to a spiritual quality of work is love (2 Cor. 5:14). Anything less corrupts quality. In the absence of love, the work may appear strong and lovely to human eyes. But when the fires of judgment and of time strike, it will be consumed. Work that is loveless is "wood, hay or stubble."

I sat stunned as a man told me that my work was mostly bricks made of straw. Sweep away the thin layer of clay and the destructibility of it all was clearly visible, he said. He was quite right. The fires of time left little of what I had been seeing as my success. All that remains is the gold the Lord himself had mined and refined amid the clay and straw (1 Cor. 3:13). The gold is in the lives of people I loved and in whom I let the Holy Spirit work.

Fifth, *God judges the man and his work separately* (1 Cor. 3:14–15).

It is important for us to see ourselves as separate from our work. A person must not evaluate himself on the basis of the church's or the project's success or failure. Success or failure of a church or work depends on several factors, including the spiritual quality of the worker's work (1 Cor. 3); the choices, works, and needs of other people involved in the work (Josh. 7); the situation in the world around the project (Hab. 3); and the sovereign design, working, and impact of God (Matt. 13:23; 1 Cor. 12:4–6). Even in the midst of a failing work, the man or woman of God may be living in harmony with the Lord and in the abundance of the beatitudes, spiritually "O.K.," prosperous, and rich toward God. Even in the midst of a corporate work that is largely "wood, hay and stubble," a faithful, loving worker may build something of solid gold.

Because a church is fundamentally a network of relationships between people and between each person and God, it may be impossible for the pastor or his evaluators to perceive him as "separate from his work." He is bound to it, emotionally and by identification.

Sometimes it is impossible to tell which is of the flesh and which is of the Spirit. So much of our work emerges from a mixture of love and selfish ambition, of spiritual power and carnal effort to prove our worth. The fires are necessary to cleanse away the carnal and worldly and to expose the spiritual and eternal.

> . . . the Day will bring it to light. It will be revealed with fire, and the fire will test the quality of each man's work. If what he has built survives, he will receive his reward. If it is burned up, he will suffer loss; *he himself will be saved*, but only as one escaping through the flames (1 Cor. 3:13–15, italics added).

Personal salvation does not depend on the effectiveness or purity of our work, but on the grace of God extended on the basis of trust in Christ (Eph. 2:8–9).

HOLD UP YOUR HEAD. YOU'RE A KING!

Even the most menial work can be a royal experience of identification with Christ—a success.

Of the lowliest Christian engaged in the merest of work, the New Testament says, "Christ . . . has made us to be kings and priests to serve his God and Father" (Rev. 1:6). "You are a chosen people, a royal priesthood," declares the apostle Peter (1 Peter 2:9). Either those are dream words without substance or they describe the reality of the lives of ordinary disciples. If position is success, we've got it!

My co-worker Kent Everhart had been in retail management and owned a successful company by the time he was twenty-one. He left it behind to concentrate on the study and teaching of the Scriptures. To make a living he did odd jobs, yard work, and freelance landscaping. One day while working at his job, which included picking up other people's trash in an apartment complex, he remembered that he was a king and a priest. He saw himself engaged in the same work Jesus does as King and Priest—cleaning up people's lives. He felt a new identification with the Lord. Menial service became a rare experience of oneness with Christ. He felt rich and successful.

It's not a mind-game we play. It is reality. With Jesus, we *are* kings and priests. That doesn't carry with it any assurance that we will be "boss," but it does give us a place of significance in the realm of God. It gives us strategic work to do. Royal service.

CHOOSE SUCCESS!

Success is to live with God's blessing; failure is to try to live without it.

In Psalm 1, success (blessing) depends on two choices. The first is to reject outright the wisdom of the godless, the way of life of the sinner, and the arrogant cynicism of the wicked (v. 1). The second is to delight (take pleasure and desire[19]) in the law of the Lord so much that you talk to yourself (mutter[20]) about it day and night (v. 2), constantly wrestling with how to apply it to daily living. If a person cares that much about his relationship with God, God promises to look out for him (v. 6). Such a person is declared successful (blessed), which means to flourish like a tree by the river, to be fruitful, to stay healthy and alive, to prosper (vv. 2–3).

It is liberating to discover that, before God, what counts as success is to believe him, love his Word, and be responsive to him. With hearts set on God, we are rich beyond words, prosperous, fortunate, blessed—successful.

I've discovered in this study that much of the pain I've suffered as a workman in God's field has been a result of worshiping the success god of the world, and always falling short of his expectations, with no hope of redemption except the agonizing effort to "do it more perfectly next time."

In my ministry I have always seemed to have two sets of goals: (1) *spiritual* goals as defined by Scripture, and (2) *carnal* goals as defined by my neurotic need for success in my own eyes and affirmation from the "significant others" in my life. With my mind and lips I may confess number 1, but number 2 is always there in my emotions. It's a duplicity that can drive a man crazy!

I am captivated by Jesus' ideas. There's something magnetic about the kind of success he offers. But when I approach my own work, I slide so easily into the world's mindset. I want my peers to think well of me. I want to leave behind some visible evidence that I was here, that is, a burgeoning church. But when the church I once pastored was buried, that left me feeling like a poor, broken-down, defeated failure—perhaps even under the curse of God!

Until I read Jesus and Paul.

There I discovered that the kind of success I'd been

looking for to prove my value is fragile and fleeting and flammable. The numbers, the impact of my ministry, and the harvest were all things that are in God's hands. I succeed, in reality, when I live my life rich toward God, available to be reshaped into his Son's likeness, willing to let the glory be his, thankful and content simply to have him and to be known by him as one of his.

The overriding emphasis in the New Testament is that success, prosperity, fulfillment, and blessedness focus mainly on what we are becoming as persons.

> True success in the biblical sense invariably has to do with inward character qualities. . . . If your motive is money, fame, or personal glory, you're not headed for success, you're headed for disappointment—even if you attain what you're seeking. But if the deepest desire of your heart is to glorify God, you're headed for real success.   —*John MacArthur*[21]

Notes

1. Lawrence O. Richards, *Expository Dictionary of Bible Words* (Grand Rapids: Zondervan, 1985), 130.
2. R. Laird Harris, *Theological Wordbook of the Old Testament* (Chicago: Moody Press, 1980), 1:132.
3. *The Amplified Bible* (Grand Rapids: Zondervan, 1965) footnote, 615.
4. Richards, *Expository Dictionary of Bible Words*, 130–131.
5. Ibid., 259.
6. Robert Young, *Analytical Concordance to the Bible* (New York: Funk & Wagnalls, n.d.), 215.
7. Richards, *Expository Dictionary of Bible Words*, 208.
8. Ibid., 207.
9. Lloyd John Ogilvie, *A Life Full of Surprises* (Nashville: Abingdon, 1969), 15.
10. J. B. Phillips, *The New Testament in Modern English* (New York: Macmillan, 1960): Matt. 5:5—"Happy are those who claim nothing . . ."
11. Ogilvie, *A Life Full of Surprises*, 24.
12. William Barclay, *Matthew*, vol. 1 (Philadelphia: Westminster, 1975), 99–100.
13. Ibid., 103.

14. Dietrich Bonhoeffer, *The Cost of Discipleship* (New York: Macmillan, 1963), 125.
15. Ogilvie, *A Life Full of Surprises*, 49.
16. Bonhoeffer, *The Cost of Discipleship*, 127.
17. Lawrence O. Richards, *Complete Bible Handbook* (Waco, Tex.: Word Books, 1987), 414–15.
18. Richards, *Expository Dictionary of Bible Words* , 259.
19. Hebrew: *chepets* (Young, *Analytical Concordance to the Bible*, 242).
20. Hebrew: *hagah* (Young, *Analytical Concordance to the Bible*, 651).
21. John MacArthur, "The Measure of Success," *Second Look* 1, no. 2 (1987): 19–20.

Chapter 9

Success and the Worldly Heart

> I undertook great projects: I built houses for myself
> and planted vineyards. . . . I amassed silver and gold
> for myself. . . . I acquired . . . the delights of the heart
> of man. . . . Yet when I surveyed all that my hands
> had done and what I had toiled to achieve,
> everything was meaningless, a chasing after the wind;
> nothing was gained under the sun.
>
> —*Ecclesiastes 2:4, 8, 11*

LIKE AN UNSEEN INFESTATION of termites, worldly thinking constantly threatens to weaken and destroy the underpin-
nings of the church. Any discussion of church success and
failure, to be complete, must deal with this evil fifth column.

American Christians watched with a helpless mixture of
horror, embarrassment, and awe as God sovereignly brought
some of his highly visible media children kicking and screaming
into the cleansing light of day. For agonizing months, the

"televangelism scandals" paraded across the pages of the secular press, filling the media with juicy bits of well-founded gossip from which no Christian escaped some level of identification. The muck smeared us all!

After the third public exposé of a Christian television personality in less than a year, the cover of *The Wittenburg Door* appropriately carried a picture of Jesus crucified on a TV antenna!

I have never been impressed with the big, "successful" TV ministries. Generally they present a misshapen caricature of both the Christian gospel and the church, leaving hugely important aspects of biblical truth untouched and unmodeled while overemphasizing other aspects that are more appealing to selfish human concerns and more attractive to potential contributors. So when God chose to reveal the very human sins of the superstars, I at first couldn't find it in my heart to weep.

When Jim Bakker was exposed, I felt embarrassment, but the scandal seemed rather far removed from me and mine. When Oral Roberts predicted his own death in order to raise $8 million for his medical school, I was sure the media would react to it exactly as they did—seeing it as a highly questionable form of emotional manipulation and evidence that Christians will do anything to raise a buck.

But when Jimmy Swaggart went before his television audience to confess that he had sinned, something changed in me. I found myself identifying keenly, painfully with him.

Perhaps it was because I had just been reading Jesus' words in Mark 7:21–22:

> For from *within*, out of men's hearts, come evil thoughts, sexual immorality, theft, murder, adultery, greed, malice, deceit, lewdness, envy, slander, arrogance and folly. All these evils come from *inside* and make a man "unclean" (italics added).

I understood these words to mean that the potential for all these things lies in human nature—*my* human nature.

After Swaggart's confession, I found myself waking up in the night, thinking about the unfinished spiritual business in my own life. Every follow-up news story brought it to mind again. I have never been unfaithful to my wife. I have never been involved with a prostitute. Still . . . I dare not hold myself up in comparison with anyone who has, nor do I want to exude any hint of spiritual superiority.

Jesus made it clear that a man can look at a woman lustfully and be guilty of adultery, even though no one knows it but he (Matt. 5:28). A person can hate another and be guilty of murder, though no death blow is ever struck (1 John 3:15). A person can covet and be jealous of the possessions, advantages, accomplishments, positions, and honors of someone else and be as guilty as if he had stolen those things, even though he has never touched them (Ex. 20:17). A person may cling to prejudices, unloving attitudes and judgments, carnal sensitivities and insensitivities, purposeful paranoias, and habits of slanderous humor—all of which perpetuate distance and lack of esteem, and sow dissension between people (Prov. 6:16–19).

Evil thoughts, malice, deceit, envy, slander, arrogance, and vanity are included in the same list with adultery, murder, and theft. These dire potentialities deeply infect the basic nature of human beings. Any expression of them openly or secretly, says Jesus, makes a person "unclean."

My response to the fall of the televangelists was changed. Now the memory of these disasters served to stimulate in me an intense, personal heart-searching and a renewed quest for personal holiness.

CONFUSION ABOUT THE BLESSING OF GOD

My greatest concern about the televangelist fiascoes is the confusion it reveals among Christians as to the nature of God's blessing and true success. "Great ministries" and their supporters often mistake numerical and material success for the blessing and approval of God.

At the very time these overexposed Christian superstars were engaging in the sins that would bring embarrassment and public ridicule, their ministries were enjoying "the blessing of

God" in terms of millions of dollars in contributions, corporate growth, and the personal wealth, popularity, and influence of the stars around whose charisma the work revolved. And since the ministries carried the stamp of God's approval—success and prosperity—what need was there for caution, spiritual honesty, repentance, or change? After all, God only blesses with such success pure motives and holy men.

Success before the world is not necessarily the evidence that God approves. It can be nothing more than a sign that the *world* approves.

The big media ministers do not suffer this mental muddle alone. J. I. Packer said in an editorial in *Christianity Today*, "The sickness of worshiping growth more than God is rampant!"[1] Smaller local churches are as caught in the perceptional mishmash as the big guys. The average church member and pastor are misled by the same confusion—the gross inability to distinguish between God's blessing and worldly success.

THE MIND BEHIND THE SYSTEM

The Scriptures abound with warnings and exhortations about the dangers inherent in this kind of confusion. "Don't let the world around you squeeze you into its own mould!" cried Paul in Romans 12:2, "but let God re-mould your minds from within" (PHILLIPS).

The world (Greek: *kosmos*) that Christians are to resist is not the material earth or the human beings that populate it or the things on it. There is a clandestine spirit on which the Bible focuses its concern.

The somber declaration rings out like a cosmic knell: "The whole world is under the control of the evil one" (1 John 5:19). He bears the name *kosmokrator*—world ruler.[2] Though he usually remains hidden from view, an evil mastermind who is the enemy of God and all that is his governs and organizes the systems of this world.

This master puppeteer who pulls the strings of the world's

systems is denounced by Jesus. On his way to the cross, he declared,

> Now is the time for judgment on this world; now *the prince of this world* shall be driven out (John 12:31, italics added).

"The prince of this world is coming," Jesus says in John 14:30. The cross of Christ seals his doom. For the time being, the Evil One still exercises authority over people who are responsive to him. It is illegitimate authority. No one is under obligation to obey him, but many still do. The day will come when his sentence will be completely carried out and his hold on the world will be broken forever (Rev. 20:10).

The *kosmos* includes all in the present order of things that appeals to the soul as an object of desire apart from and in rivalry to God.[3] The monetary system, educational system, political system, trade system, various systems of science and technology—all are by nature worldly. Living in this world, Christians touch these things every day. They may legitimately claim and use them for the glory of God. But when believers use law, education, medicine, money, or organization, they are to remember it is something worldly, not spiritual, that they are handling. They are in contact with Satan's realm. They are warned to use caution lest they become engrossed or entangled (1 Cor. 7:31), and they are to resist conformity to the system's inherent spirit (Rom. 12:2). They are to keep from setting their affections on anything in the realm (1 John 2:15–16). These things are part of the order Satan has built to compete with God's order. Even while they are being used for some holy purpose, they have the potential to draw us away from God.

We must take this understanding into our work and ministry for the Lord, or we will become easy prey for the termites that secretly undermine that work from within.

LOVE AFFAIR WITH THE WORLD

To fall in love with the world is to fall out of love with God. The two loves are antithetical and incompatible.

> If anyone loves the world, the love of the Father is not in him
> (1 John 2:15).

Three kinds of lust-love identify the spirit of the world
(1 John 2:16).

The lust of the flesh. To want the things that fallen human
nature wants is poison to our affection for God. Galatians 5:19
identifies some of these wants, the deeds to which they give
rise, and the dangers toward which they lead:

> Now the deeds of the flesh are evident, which are: immorality,
> impurity, sensuality, idolatry, sorcery, enmities, strife, jealousy,
> outbursts of anger, disputes, dissensions, factions, envyings,
> drunkenness, carousings, and things like these, of which I
> forewarn you just as I have forewarned you that those who
> practice such things shall not inherit the kingdom of God (NASB).

These wants-works represent the natural direction people
take without the "hindering" (Gal. 5:17) of the Holy Spirit, who
alone is the source of adequate energy to resist the seduction of
the world. These deeds titillate and tantalize the imagination.
The mind behind the system is bent on reshaping our minds
until we approve rather than disapprove such things. The
secular media bombard us with deceptive propaganda. Exposed as we are to the world's mindset, it is easy for sensitivity
to certain sins to be numbed. If we are honest, we can detect
places where we have made subtle compromises with the
world's priorities and values. Lack of fundamental awareness of
the points at which we are dealing with the world leaves us
especially vulnerable.

The lust of the eyes. "The lust which the eye begets by
seeing."[4] The serpent shows Eve the fruit. She sees it as "good
for food." The lust resulting from looking at the forbidden fruit
contributes to her moral collapse. The devil takes Jesus to a
high place and shows him all the kingdoms of the world. He is
tempted to give allegiance to the enemy in order to win for
himself all he can see with his eyes. He resists every form of
temptation with the sword of God's recorded Word. The enemy
flees.

Modern Christian eyes see much to draw us away from God. So many stimuli, so many things to look at that appeal to greed and impurity and sensuality and spiritual carelessness! Many worldly things become increasingly irresistible the longer we stand wide-eyed and *look*.

The pride of life. This includes everything that appeals to carnal human pride: position, notoriety, ownership, influence, success, and beauty. The world's thinking is that personal worth, a good self-image, well-being, meaning, and happiness require such things. In its cosmic confusion, even Christendom sees them as essential evidences of the blessing of God. The Scriptures, by contrast, promise well-being and fulfillment only from receptiveness to God's mercies, obedience to his will, assurance of eternal life, a life of living sacrifice to God, and personal character reshaped to be godlike.

Sometimes worldly success surprises us. Yesterday we were unknown; today everyone is clamoring to see and hear us. Yesterday we struggled to make ends meet; today plenty of money is coming our way. Yesterday no opportunity for worldly success seemed to exist; today doors are opening to power, influence, and prosperity. Mistaking what we see from this unfamiliar "high place" as the blessing of God, we may become deceived and be swept away, not by the Holy Spirit but by the spirit of the age. The true blessing of God becomes diluted and we don't know it. Believing that prosperity and the blessing of God are the same thing, we arrogantly think God approves of everything we do. Our pride blinds us to the truth that much we are counting as success is, in reality, of no more value than manure![5]

Something happened recently that helped me understand a little better how easily the pride of life can turn my heart from God.

For us Girards, church choir is a family affair—I sing bass, Audrey sings soprano, our teenage daughter Charity sings alto. Last fall the choir sang a gospel song called "Satisfied." Charity had the solo on the second verse. After we sang it for the church, the song went through my mind over and over. I found myself singing it constantly and being disturbed by the truth about me it exposed.

> I'm not rich in great possessions,
>   but in the smallness of my wants,
> I'm satisfied, completely satisfied.
> The world can offer all it wants to;
>   I only have this one response,
> I'm satisfied, completely satisfied.
> My soul cries out: Hallelujah! I've found him,
>   Whom for so long my spirit
>   had wished and longed and craved!
> *I have Jesus! Could I ask for anything more?*
> I'm satisfied, completely satisfied.[6]

I was disturbed because, as the musical question rolled over in my mind, I was shocked to discover that I often am *not* satisfied with Jesus. I am asking for more, expecting more. I've been looking in other places for my sense of self-worth. This keeps me *dissatisfied*, because I keep expecting people, the Christian community, personal achievements, and relationships to satisfy the craving for approval and worthiness. It doesn't work. None of those things is able to give the lasting satisfaction, affirmation, well-being, and joy that Jesus Christ, by his acceptance and lordship, can supply. Carnal pride is never satisfied. The more I seek to find satisfaction in accomplishments about which I can boast, the more I distance myself from the real thing.

The pride of life can also be expressed in an independent approach to ministry. A spirit of nonaccountability characterizes Christians and ministries that do not really see the body and their place in it. Separateness as Christians and Christian works is a worldly, not a spiritual, attitude.

RESULTS OF FALLING IN LOVE WITH THE WORLD

The results of a love affair with the world are at first nearly undetectable, but ultimately grow into full-fledged tragedy.

Love for God erodes as love-lust for the world increases (1 John 2:15). The change is subtle and progressive. It starts as a seed, then develops a root, then becomes a full-grown tree bearing bad fruit.

"The love of money," says 1 Timothy 6:10, is the root of evil. So is the love of publicity and notoriety, the love of property and position, the love of enterprise and prosperity, the love of power and influence, and the love of great public and religious works. The natural appeal of these things is tremendous . . . and *natural.*

For a while the two loves seem to coexist. That is part of the deception. But before long it becomes apparent that one's worldly attachments and commitments are squeezing out attachment and commitment to God. The Bible likens the process to the dynamics of a marriage ravaged by adultery. Seizing the analogy, James cries, "You adulterous people, don't you know that friendship with the world is hatred toward God? Anyone who chooses to be a friend of the world becomes an enemy of God" (James 4:4).

Love-lust for the world chokes normal spiritual growth. In his parable of the sower Jesus told how some gospel seed falls among the thorns. Thorns and gospel seed try to grow up together, but the thorns eventually choke the life out of the good seed. In his explanation (Luke 8:14), Jesus said that the seed among the thorns represents people who really listen to the gospel, make a start in response to it, but "they never mature" (BERKELEY), because the word is choked by the attachments and demands of the world—namely, "worries and wealth and pleasures of life."

Because of a continuing love affair with the system and its advantages, some Christians simply never grow up. They may have talents and personal charisma that keep them in the public eye, bring them prosperity, and make them *seem* wise. But they never come to spiritual adulthood, because their growth is choked by continuing love-lust for the arrangements of the world.

Love-lust for the world always corrupts. The Bible uses words like "stained," "blemished," "spotted" (James 1:27); "corruption," "decay," "ruin," "mortality," "depravity" (2 Peter 1:4); "pollution," "defilement" (2 Peter 2:20)[7] to describe the effect of intercourse with the world on the lives of persons. Second Peter 2:20 insists that it is possible for people who have escaped the world's corruption through knowing Jesus Christ to become entangled in it again and eventually to be overcome by it— ending up worse off than they were at the beginning. No one who dabbles in affection for worldly ways and advantages escapes unscathed by it. It leaves its ugly mark on both the person and his work. Unfaced, unrepented of, it can bring us to spiritual ruin.

Love-lust for the world undermines Christian relationships and loyalties. In 2 Timothy 4, Paul urges Timothy to come to him. The paragraph resonates with loneliness and rejection, especially one sentence: "Demas, *because he loved this world,* has deserted me and gone to Thessalonica" (v. 10). Relationships between Christians are described in Scripture as kinship in God's household (Mark 11:30; Eph. 2:19), as interdependent parts placed by the Holy Spirit into Christ's body (1 Cor. 12:12–27), and as living stones built together by the Spirit into a living temple the Lord fills with his presence (Eph. 2:20–22; 1 Peter 2:5).

The fundamental ties are *spiritual,* not fleshly or worldly. As time goes by we become attached as best friends and allies, but the thing that holds us together is the Spirit we share in common. Love for the world undermines that spiritual bond. As our affections drift away from God, our relationships with each other start to come apart. It may begin with marriage problems, or it may show up in strained ties with church members or co-workers. We become taken with ourselves—*our* needs, *our* satisfaction, *our* pleasure, *our* success—and little by little our loyalty to our spiritual kin disappears.

Be on guard! A vision of a great work for God, designed to keep it unimpeded by the need to be accountable to one's spiritual peers, may in its independence of spirit contain the warning signs of a growing love affair with the world.

TESTS OF A TRUE MINISTRY

One of the documents of the early church contains a listing of what to look for in a prophet—how to tell whether he or she is real or bogus. The *Didache* says that if the prophet asks for money, don't listen to him! The apostle Paul says,

> When I came to you, brothers, I did not come with eloquence or superior wisdom as I proclaimed to you the testimony about God. For I resolved to know nothing while I was with you except Jesus Christ and him crucified. I came to you in weakness and fear, and with much trembling. My message and my preaching were not with wise and persuasive words, but with a demonstration of the Spirit's power, so that your faith might not rest on men's wisdom, but on God's power (1 Cor. 2:1–5).

The early Christians expected their ministries to be altogether free of worldly attachments. A work was recognized as blessed of God if the Holy Spirit was its source of power. If the energy for the work was Spirit-power, not only the work but also the quality of the workers' lives would be miraculous. Two kinds of spiritual fruit would be visible: changed lives, including new converts (John 4:35; 15:16), and the development of Christlike character dominated by love (Gal. 5:22–23).

In addition, the thinking that pervaded the process would be different from that which defines all worldly projects. If it paralleled the world's values too closely, it was a mere work of men. If the wisdom of God were its controlling principle, humility, transparency, and honesty would distinguish the workers as they worked. Their admitted weaknesses would enhance the working of God. The accepted standards of evaluation would be useless in measuring the effectiveness and power of the project. The wise of the world might miss the point of such a ministry. The powers that be and the prevailing culture are likely to oppose it. The world may consider it unwise, imprudent, foolish, unsuccessful. Christians tuned to earthly wisdom may rate it unblessed.

But the power of God would be there, apparent in growing

faithfulness, godliness, and loving service—the divine measures of success in ministry and manhood.

Notes

1. J. I. Packer, "Nothing Fails Like Success," *Christianity Today* (12 August 1988): 15.
2. A word used only once in the New Testament, in Ephesians 6:12, in reference to his demonic lieutenants, "world rulers of this darkness."
3. J. R. Dummelow, *A Commentary on the Holy Bible* (New York: Macmillan, 1923), 1056.
4. Henry Alford, *The New Testament for English Readers* (1893; reprint, Chicago: Moody Press, 1976), 1709.
5. Philippians 3:4–9, KJV.
6. Steve Adams, "Satisfied" (Copyright © 1978 by Steve Adams Music/ASCAP. International copyright secured. All rights controlled by Franklin House, P.O. Box 989, Franklin, TN 37064).
7. Harold K. Moulton, *Analytical Greek Lexicon*, rev. ed. (Grand Rapids: Zondervan, 1978), 269, 425.

Chapter 10

Leaping Into the Crowd

> When koinonia is restored to the life of the church,
> leadership is bound to change radically. Once a
> community of faith tastes the discovery that the
> treasure is in the people, it will not tolerate or create
> a dependency system controlled by one leader. As we
> each experience our gifts, and the wonder of our
> value in Christ, the "chain of command" is broken.
> When we realize that the Spirit intends to work and
> speak through us too, we have to say to our former
> bosses, "I will work *with* you, but I cannot work *for*
> you."
> —*Stan Jones*[1]

AS YOU MAY HAVE already gathered, I reentered pastoral
ministry reluctantly. I had felt emasculated and prostituted by
the traditional role expectations that go with the job. Admitted-
ly, my determination not to pastor again was laden with
contradiction and conflict . . . and not a little guilt. I love to

preach. Always have, always will. I am thoroughly convinced that no healthy Christian can really exist outside the body of Christ. So I am bound to be in the church. I am and I want to be a lover of people and of God. My greatest fulfillment in life has come from the study and teaching of the Word and the shepherding of God's flock. At the same time, I feel that the shepherd life robbed me of too many things that are important to a healthy sense of personhood, and I was left wounded and bleeding from unwarranted attacks from both sheep and wolves.

If there was to be any place for me in ministry, it would have to be as a needy brother among the brothers.

THE SECRET POWER OF SERVANT-LEADERSHIP

Jesus has told us there is power in the "among-and-beside them" position that can never be experienced while "over-and-above them." He says in Matthew 20:25–28 that leadership in the church is not the same as leadership in the world. It is unique. Kingdom leadership is not patterned after the styles of business, professional, political, or military leaders.

The authority structure of the church is established on the principle of servanthood rather than leadership (as that term is usually understood). Leaders in this movement are an unusual breed of nonleaders who would rather be called servants. As servants they refuse to lord it over people, pull rank, or make the demands of their office (v. 25). The best leaders are those who serve not their own needs, but the needs of those in their care (v. 27). Like Jesus, they are willing to give their lives, pouring their souls out for those they serve (v. 28, NASB margin).

There is no hierarchy in the church. Christian leaders are not to see themselves in any sense above those they lead. This seems clear from Jesus' instructions in Matthew 23:1–12. He tells his disciples not to act like Pharisees: "Everything they do is done for men to see: . . . they love the place of honor at banquets and the most important seats in the synagogues; they love to be greeted in the marketplaces and to have men call them 'Rabbi.' " (All the wrong reasons for seeking leadership in the church!)

"Do not do what they do," Jesus says.

In verses 8 and 9 Jesus gets specific: "You are not to be called 'Rabbi' [teacher], for you have only one Master and you are all brothers. And do not call anyone on earth 'father,' for you have one Father, and he is in heaven." (Don't try to give a brother the place of a father.)

Today Jesus might have added: "Do not call anyone on earth 'Reverend,' for only God in heaven is worthy of reverence—'Holy and reverend is *his* name' " (Ps. 111:9, KJV, italics added).

Only the NASB dares to translate Matthew 23:10 as it is in the original: "And do not be called *leaders;* for one is your Leader, that is, Christ. But the greatest among you shall be your servant" (italics added). The primary meaning of the original word is not "teacher" or "master" as it is rendered in most translations, but "leader."

This is a difficult instruction from the Lord. Who of us has ever observed anything like Jesus' scheme of brother-servant leadership? Most people seem to be looking for leaders they can idolize, who will lord it over them, decide what is right for them, and take the responsibility. We respond readily to the leadership of a father, but it is difficult to accept direction from one who insists he is a brother, an equal.

The Bible seems to contradict itself at this point. On the list of spiritual equipment of the body of Christ in Romans 12:6–8, there is a gift called "leadership": "If a man's gift is . . . leadership, let him govern diligently."

The Greek word for "leadership" means to be appointed over, to preside, to govern, to superintend, and to give aid.[2] The spiritual gift of leadership is expressed in an aid-giving ministry that helps the church make spiritual progress.

Jesus says we must not covet the designation "leader" if that means to seek a place higher than others in the church. And yet there is a *service of leading* which is a body necessity and for which individuals are equipped by the Holy Spirit. The apparent tension between these two ideas is resolved if, in the exercises of this ministry, the one thus gifted and those he serves always see Christ as leader and the gifted One as one among the brothers.

What the Christian leader is to avoid is "exercising authority" (Matt. 20:25). The original Greek word is a nearly unpronounceable verb meaning to get in one's power, to bring under, to master or control, to overcome, to dominate.[3] Larry Richards says the word implies a tendency toward whatever compulsion is required to gain compliance.[4] Jesus says that such leadership has no place in the church.

In Matthew 23:1–12 Jesus pinpoints several aspects of leadership of the type he tells Christians to refuse to emulate: (1) they do not practice what they preach (v. 3); (2) they place burdens on others that they themselves refuse to carry (v. 4); (3) they cherish recognition and acceptance. To be perceived as spiritual leaders they put on religious piety just for show. They engage in "spiritual activities" they scarcely believe in so as to keep their coveted positions (v. 5); (4) they love the places of honor that go with the office—seating at the head table, the power of the pulpit, public recognition, marching at the front of sacred processions (vv. 6–7); (5) they covet titles of respect such as "Rabbi," "Father," "Doctor," "Bishop," "Elder," "Pastor" (vv. 7, 9–10).

There is authentic spiritual authority which properly functions in the church. The word Paul uses for it is not the same one used to describe worldly leadership. Paul's word is *exousia* (in 2 Corinthians 10:8, for example), meaning ability, liberty, license, rule, dominion, jurisdiction.[5] This has nothing to do with putting others down so we can gain power over them. Rather, it indicates a license or freedom to lead.

The focus of this jurisdictional style is a clear contrast to the world's exercise of authority. The Lord gives his servant-leaders authority "for building you up, not tearing you down" (2 Cor. 10:8; 13:10). The authority of true servant-leaders is strictly limited to building people up.

In 2 Corinthians 13:10 Paul expresses concern not to be "harsh in the use of authority." Some Christians refused to acknowledge that Christ was speaking through Paul. His response was to remind them that "Christ is not weak in dealing with you, but is powerful *among you!*" (13:3). No need to belittle, manipulate, or threaten. The leader's confidence is based on his faith that Jesus is alive and active in his people. If they do what he asks them to do, it is because they know Jesus himself is speaking and caring for them through his servant-leader.

One is your leader: Christ! Whatever authority Christian servant-leaders have does not include the right to control the actions and choices of their brothers and sisters. The only legitimate authority we have is to help people follow Christ.

The one who serves the body of Christ with the gift of leadership in a true and honest way will not covet high position and will not allow people to idolize or deify him. Whether they like it or not, he will trash his "hero button" and climb down from his phony, elevated perch in order to sit as a mere man with mere men, to be the lowliest of brothers among his brothers. He will wash their feet if need be, in order to be, not the "master know-it-all," but a servant in the royal priesthood of believers—just like any other Christian.

This is not a role the church readily accepts for its pastors. My experience is that it is a place in the kingdom that may have to be taken by force![6]

AT HOME WITH STRANGERS

We shouldn't have felt at home in the only church in Lake Montezuma, Arizona. We were surrounded by septuagenarians and octogenarians! At forty-eight Audrey and I were the youngest people present, and our sixth-grader, Charity, was the only child.

"Around here," Sam Wrona told me, "you're just a kid!"

The services were "country formal." The pastor, who was in his seventies, drove in on Sundays from another town to preach a simple gospel message. The "nondenominational" congregation knew nothing of the foment of ecclesiastical renewal in which we had been living for fifteen years.

The first Sunday after tucking ourselves into our tiny trailer cottage, we found our way to the corner of Rusty Spurs and Drifting Sands roads and the little brown A-frame called "Montezuma Chapel." When visitor's cards were distributed, in response to the question, "Would you like the pastor to visit you?" I wrote, "Yes." To "Would you like to become a member of this church?" I answered, "I already am a member of the body of Christ. So naturally I want to become involved in any way I can with my brothers and sisters here."

Two days later, the pastor came to see us. I did not tell him I had ever been a pastor, ever written a religious book, or ever had "Rev." in front of my name. No one in town knew it. I was not going to let anyone know. Looking back on that first pastoral visit, I think the old preacher knew in spite of my precautions. Months later, after I had accepted the church's call, he told Audrey and me, "When I saw that visitor's card, I knew the replacement I'd been praying for had arrived!"

The only class in the Sunday school, the adult class, was without a teacher. In spite of my warning that he was taking a terrible risk, the pastor urged me to accept the job.

Next Sunday, I found myself in a classroom with a dozen strangers who had just begun to study the book of Acts. They were at about chapter 4. "Before I get into Acts with you, I feel like we need to get to know one another," I said. "I feel it's important not only to learn the contents of the Bible, but to learn to love each other, so we can relate Scripture to our lives and relationships. So, with study we will also do some personal sharing."

It took two Sundays to get through "the Quaker Questions":

> Between the ages of seven and twelve . . .
> Where did you live?
> How many brothers and sisters did you have?

How did you heat your house?
Where was the center of human warmth in your home?
When did God become more than just a word to you?

Something fresh and exciting began to happen. People, many of whom thought they'd seen it all, began to experience a new kind of relationship in church. Then we turned to the book of Acts, continuing to structure the class sessions to keep the relational focus. And the quality of fellowship pictured in the New Testament began to break over the group like sunrise.

I knew . . . we were home.

REJECTED AGAIN

The editor's phone call left me angry and numb. This was my third rejection notice in less than a year!

I had spent nearly two years researching the current writing project. I had hoped its publication would open a place for me as a full-time writer. The editors decided that the book was not what they wanted, and one of them called with the news. Not only would the work of two years be scrapped, but royalty advance payments would stop, throwing our already shaky family finances into chaos.

In a few hours, depression would eat me up, continue its morbid feast for several days, then return with regularity.

Mature faith could have supplied the vision that all of this was "God at work." Instead, deep doubts concerning my personal worth gave birth to intense feelings of failure, feelings that would have to be wrestled down before that kind of faith could be mustered.

Failure!

Another in the outrageous series! If I doubted it before, now I knew for certain: *Bob Girard, you are a dismal failure!*

What I did not know was that God was at work. And his timing was perfect.

THE RELUCTANT PROPHET

Jim Summerton, the pastor, was planning a month's vacation. He asked if I would preach the four Sundays he was gone. I still had not told him about my past. But the opportunity to preach was irresistible.

'I can't take the second Sunday," I told him. "I have to be in Seattle. But I'll take the other three."

"Fine. I'll come back for the second Sunday," he said.

The first Sunday of the pastor's vacation, I preached the first of three sermons on Jonah the Reluctant Prophet. Wednesday, the editor's devastating phone call came. Friday, I flew to Seattle to fulfill my commitment.

The second Sunday of his vacation, the pastor returned, preached, and . . . *resigned!*

The third Sunday of the pastor's vacation, I preached the second of three sermons on Jonah the Reluctant Prophet. And found myself answering the question, "Will you consider replacing Jim Summerton as pastor of the church?"

I had been set up!

I told them about my past failures in the pastorate, about my revulsion to certain responsibilities, and about how I came to Lake Montezuma to get as far away from those things as possible. I told them about being in therapy. I hoped they would decide I was too spiritually and emotionally crippled to do them any good. I told them everything but no—because I sincerely did not want to be saying no to God.

The fourth Sunday of the pastor's vacation, I preached the third sermon on Jonah the Reluctant Prophet. And some people in the church were already thinking of me as "the new pastor."

LYSTRA REVISITED

Monday night following my third Reluctant Prophet sermon, I attended a potluck dinner sponsored by the Chapel Guild. It was horrible. The hostess insisted I sit at the "head table," the most abominable seat in any Christian gathering—

reserved, evidently, for people who are too good for anyone to talk to, since no one is ever seated across from you. This arrangement gives everyone in the room a clear view of each tomato-soaked tidbit dribbling down your chin. You feel like you have to watch every move you make lest you slip below the expectations that attach to anyone wonderful enough to be seated in such a place of "honor."

Of course, now that I was known by all as "pastor material," no one in the room could possibly be called upon to pray but me!

People who had been my friends before they found out about the subhuman nature of what I really am now spoke to me with greater care (and greater dishonesty).

I came home drained, empty, and angry, seriously wondering if I belonged in that church at all. Hurting, I wrote my feelings, in order to sort them out.

My three Sundays of preaching have totally "blown my cover." I am, in the minds of many, the new guru they've been looking for. There is a group determined to mount me on their pastoral pedestal, high above the rest of humanity, where they can pull my sanctimonious strings, push my holy buttons and watch me dance the deadly "pastoral fling" right into the chains from which I have only so recently slipped free.

It's no fun any more!

Laymen have fun. Pastors don't. I don't want to be pastor again if that's the price tag on it. By God! I won't give up my manhood again to be a pine-scented Pinocchio whose nose grows longer, whose strings grow tighter every time he accepts the deceitful, lying mask which is, more than anything else, the badge of his profession!

I woke up this morning with my feelings of resentment pretty well identified. Angry that I had allowed myself to be put into that damnable iron maiden of role expectations without fighting it. Angry at my "fans" for pushing me to it. And seriously doubting if I had any business even considering a return to the pulpit and pastorate.

My mind began casting about for something from Scripture to speak to the issue. Paul and Barnabas' success and problems at Lystra came to mind (Acts 14:8–19) . . .

Through Paul's preaching, a lame man believed Jesus could heal him. Paul discerned the reality of the man's faith and encouraged him to act on it. The cripple jumped up and began to walk. The crowd of pagans who had been watching thought Paul and Barnabas had done this wonderful thing by their personal power.

"The gods have come down to us in human form!" the people concluded.

It was a devilish diversion. Instead of being a thing to God's glory, the people's appreciation became idolatry, a diabolically inspired act of rebellion against God! A complete misunderstanding of the truth. A lie!

When the apostles heard it, they took drastic action to halt the spread of this devilish doctrine. They tore their clothes to rags and plunged into the "appreciative" crowd shouting the truth:

"Why are you doing this? We too are only men, human—like you!"

They renounced the lie, the falsely founded accolades, and the "over you" position the people were insisting on for them. They knocked down and shattered the pedestal to which appreciative people had lifted them against their will and against God's will.

They dared to call the "great honor" the people gave them a "worthless thing" which must be repudiated in order to come to God!

Paul and Barnabas were exercising true servant-leadership when they tore off their clothes and plunged into the crowd. Apostolic authenticity required them to reject and forsake the exalted places which had been constructed for them, so they could come down among the people, where they could be touched and viewed at close range. The error about who they really were could not be tolerated. In a desperate and imprudent demonstration they became naked and fully visible, so that there could be no mistake that they were flesh and blood—ordinary humanity.

Their vulnerability nearly cost them their lives!

Returning to Lystra on their way home to Antioch several months later, they put their actions in eternal perspective: "We must go through many hardships to enter the kingdom of God" (Acts 14:22).

The choice is mine, isn't it, Lord. I can let these people flatter me and elevate me and confine me to that lonely pedestal. I can let them thank me when they should be thanking God. I can let them depend on me when they should be trusting the Holy Spirit. I can go along with their error at this point, but the cost will be very dear: The kingdom of God, the experience of the new community Jesus came to establish, will be missed because of deceitful and worldly folly.

I'm not sure exactly how, in this place, to tear off my clothes, plunge into the crowd and demand to be known and related to as human, or how to help them see the worthlessness of their dehumanizing idolatry. Most of the church world is woefully trapped in the same deadly sin. And my pride is extremely susceptible to permitting this idolatry to go on.

The freedom I've found these past three hardship-filled years will be pirated away if I do not win this war within myself. I must be free. I must be a man. Or nothing I try to do will be anything but a slavery of lies.

After six weeks of struggling, equivocating, and praying, I reluctantly gave the church permission to present my name to the congregation for a vote. The Sunday before the vote a strange change came over me—I crossed a line. As I led the morning worship service and preached, I felt as if I was already the pastor of the church.

FOOT-DRAGGING

Even so, for three years after accepting the church's call, the questions, doubts, and distaste for it persisted. I was not sure it was what I really wanted to do. The old feelings of resentment and inadequacy constantly disrupted my attitudes toward the work.

I consciously limited the intensity of my commitment. For three years, most of my sermons came from "the barrel." I had my hands full building our house, I told myself. No time to try to ascertain specific local needs and to speak to them unless they happened to coincide with something I had previously preached on the subject.

I was glad for my "part-time" status. It gave me an excuse to say no and to sidestep pastoral responsibilities I considered distasteful. In the back of my mind—and often up front—I hoped I would soon be able to escape again into some other job or calling.

While most of the congregation was accepting and patient, some clung to traditional pastoral expectations that I was either unwilling or emotionally incapable of fulfilling. For example, I was a disappointment to those who expected me to be there whenever anyone was sick. Others in the church were well equipped to visit, pray, and care for the sick, and they did so with effectiveness and joy. There was no need for me to go too. Besides, I was still struggling with my own inner sickness. This led to some painful confrontations and attrition in the church.

A major issue from the beginning has been the length of the Sunday services. Many felt that anything over sixty minutes was a gross imposition and a breach of all the laws of religious propriety. Some argued it was a health hazard for older people to spend more than an hour in church. I insisted such limits were unbiblical, unspiritual, inconsistent, and impossible, given the kinds of things that need to be done in Christian meetings. I felt the whole issue was the height of silliness and rigidity and a point where Christians needed to stop being babies and grow up. I faced gentle-to-bitter criticism after nearly every service and especially at meetings of the church boards. I tried to accommodate to the complaining, but usually found it impossible to keep the meetings within the desired limits. I suggested the church fire me (and hoped they would). They refused to take the bait.

As changes came in the worship format and a participatory style of meeting developed, the Sunday service only lengthened, and brittle souls howled in pain and pulled out. It was an issue that would not go away. Finally, to keep the body together and provide freedom for people to make their own spiritual choices, we have come to a two-hour "worship-celebration" with a coffee break in the middle, so that those who cannot abide such a fellowship marathon can escape.

The confrontations triggered by these expectational frustrations set off familiar negative responses that lay not-quite-dormant just under my skin. With soul-numbing regularity, I was ready again to cut and run, to leave this stupid and needless pain behind, and find peace in doing something else with my life.

"Lord," I screamed, "I didn't want this job in the first place, and I still don't want it. Why do I have to be a *pastor?*"

Another journal entry:

John Woodson asked this morning if I was thinking about quitting the ministry. I told him I'd been thinking about it for twenty-five years!

You'd think I'd grow out of it. But I don't. The pain is always there. The sense of rejection because I can't please some people whose voices carry weight in the church. The sense of loneliness because the people I think are important don't give me the unqualified support I think I need. The sense of betrayal. They say I've let them down. I say they have let me down!

God! You once seemed to be telling me that it was okay for me to leave the ministry. But you shoved me back in. You knew I'd be at this place again—depressed, wanting out, wishing for death, hurting, desperate. You knew! and still you suckered me into this.

Can't you see, God . . . I am not the man for this job! There must be someone else! Can the church only be born in this place if I travail in these unwanted labor pains?

HOSPITAL FOR A WOUNDED PREACHER

At the core of the church was a knot of struggling believers who, though unaware of their healing power, became a convalescent hospital for me. Many were uncertain about the basics of salvation, the leadership of the Spirit, and the will of God, and few thought of themselves as priests or ministers with anything to share that could help another Christian survive and grow. Yet, by being themselves they became a therapeutic team carrying me through the finishing stages of emotional and spiritual rehabilitation.

The expectations of most were quite low. (I couldn't have survived the return to active ministry if they had expected much.) They accepted me as a human being. They suffered with my weaknesses and the ugliness of my wounds. They affirmed my preaching and responded to the minimal leadership I tried to give. I have never been anywhere where there was such consistent expression of appreciation for my ministry. The baby Christians of Montezuma Chapel treated me as if I were God's gift to them. They gave me time to find myself in ministry again. Few really understood the fear and reluctance with which I was struggling, but the Spirit-born fruit of patience was in them.

Patience and affirmation, patience and affirmation.

I began to know I was loved and could dare to love back. Confidence in my gifts was restored, along with the clear sense that in the strategy of God, even with my record of failure and brokenness, there was nonetheless a place for me.

It was precisely the kind of environment my ragged spiritual state required, if I was ever to find my way to peace in the work.

THE MIRACULOUS POWER OF THE PREACHED WORD

I was the reluctant prophet, spit out onto the beach, preaching God's Word, not because I wanted to, but because "woe is me if I preach not!" I didn't want to care as much as I had in the past. I didn't want to involve myself that deeply with people. I wanted to be a nice guy and to be appreciated, but I wasn't at all sure I wanted to really love anybody.

And yet I found myself loving these people in spite of my self-protective intentions. I often call this community "Terminal City," because so many people are dying. In the tradition of the American retirement system, many have come here to wait for death. There are families with children, but more people in this town are closer to death than in any group I've ever lived and worked with. Whether my neighbors and friends are Christians or not, I can't help hurting with their struggles. I weep when they weep. I struggle with them to find answers to sickness, death, pain, and heartbreak. I groan with them when the answers are hard to find. I die with them when they die. And I grieve with their families. In spite of my reluctance.

Through nearly three decades of preaching, I had filed my sermon manuscripts away. Now I pulled them out of the file, dusted them off, and read them to my new flock. I did not have the heart to prepare new ones. What I preached was the truth: mostly expositions of Scripture, sound biblical doctrine, including New Testament ecclesiology (principles of church life).

And then I was surprised when the Word began to bear fruit! Some people said, "Give us more!" And their lives began to demonstrate authentic spiritual growth. New spiritual confidence began to be expressed. Fear of talking about one's faith began to disappear. Changes came in their relationships with one another. There had always been a readiness to help one another in neighborly ways, but now some began to speak of love for each other. Natural barriers to acceptance and caring began to be faced and penetrated. And some began to press the issues my sermonic "retreads" were raising. "Let's become a more biblical kind of a church!" they said.

The only changes that had been made to that point were a few adjustments in the Sunday meeting toward a more informal and personal style, and the development of a few, small home "growth groups," where people studied the Bible, shared what was happening in their lives, prayed, and gained personal experience in body life.

I found myself the fidgety participant in another process of church renewal, with an intriguing twist—I was the one with the worried look, saying, "Now wait a minute! Let's not be in too much of a hurry."

THE GENTLER PROCESS OF RADICAL CHANGE

There is more to servant-leadership than being reluctant to lead. It can be successfully argued that reluctance is not one of the more desirable characteristics of a true servant. The cross is involved. Giving one's life for the flock, if need be. Willingness to suffer the very pains I was so determined not to suffer again. But reluctance may not have been a bad place for me to start. It gave me time to find my way back while avoiding at least some of the old traps.

My reluctance to ascend the pastoral pedestal had at least one positive effect—it kept me from trying to be the boss and made me more ready to accept the role of brother-servant. When I led, I led from weakness—which caused others to accept responsibilities I could not or would not assume. As restoration came and love for these people grew, my reluctance decreased, and I found myself doing some "pastoral" things out of friendship and genuine caring.

My vision for shared pastoral leadership made me open to potential peer pastors the Lord sent our way. To Audrey and me, one confirmation that God had special plans for this congregation was the arrival of spiritually qualified people. From such divergent places as southern Arizona, Texas, Missouri, Iowa, Micronesia, and elsewhere, men and women have moved to this place, saying in a variety of ways, "We believe God called us to this community. He assured us that this is where we belong and that he has a ministry for us here."

When somebody makes that kind of statement, I have learned to listen with a combination of guarded excitement and healthy skepticism. But in time it became apparent that several of these were deeply committed Christians with a mature grasp of the Word of God. Among them were self-taught students of the original biblical languages. A few possessed a strong sense of the body of Christ, borne of serious biblical research and experience.

Some had suffered painful rejection by established churches. Two came almost directly from rejection by a church in the Midwest where they had dared to challenge the development of an unbiblical dictatorial authority structure. Some were returning to "organized religion" after years in house churches and were excited with the acceptance and spiritual life they found developing among us. Others had come into a sense of the body, a knowledge of the Word, and a mature Christian walk within established churches. They had developed a strong sense of individual priesthood and personal relationships with God that were stable and practical.

Out of this "gathering of eagles" has come a team of teachers, pastors, elders, and others who are learning together to provide pastoral care for this flock.

In important ways, authentic renewal—revival?—has come to Montezuma Chapel. The town's once-reputed "country club church" has become a hotbed of Bible study, caring, and spiritual growth. People who were uncertain of their salvation are sure now. People who knew practically nothing of the Word of God now study the Bible regularly. Love has begun to flourish and touch people inside and outside the core group. Younger people have been assimilated into the fellowship. Personal ministries are being discovered and pursued. The believer-priesthood is awakening. Prayer is growing in volume and power. Commitments to Christ and one another are being proved by visible actions and deepening loyalty.

A study team worked with the Scriptures and local church needs for two years to develop a new organizational and philosophical document (bylaws) incorporating spiritual church-life principles into the "official" structure of the church. It was adopted unanimously.

Many of these things represent significant (even phenomenal) changes in the church. But I hesitate to tell our story in much more detail for two reasons:

1. The metamorphosis is far from complete. Not everyone in the church and community is happy with the change. The demand to return to a more "traditional" style of church life is constantly voiced. Some "charismatics" among us may never be completely happy with our deliberate hesitancy to change

too much too quickly, giving time for love and acceptance to demonstrate itself in patience.

As a congregation we are still very much married to the institution. Real Christians are confused as to the true nature of the church. Re-education must come. By introducing precepts, by preaching, teaching, modeling, and loving, by making changes with great care and sensitivity toward persons, and by exercising wisdom from the Spirit, we pursue true spiritual, attitudinal, relational and ecclesiological renewal.

I was asked once why I choose to stay in the institution when it would be so much easier to build a New Testament quality of church life outside. "Because most of God's people are inside," I said. "I am called to stay with them and to work with them to become what God wants his church to become."

2. I don't wish to inspire copycat churches. Each congregation must grapple with the principles of New Testament ecclesiology for itself, and ask the Spirit to produce a new wineskin suitable to contain and enhance what God is doing with each particular group of believers. The variety in the way various biblical churches are described indicates a uniqueness from church to church which is much like the personal uniqueness that the gift passages affirm. The Roman church had a different configuration of ministries and gifts from the Corinthian church (Rom. 12:6–8; 1 Cor. 12:4–11). The church at Ephesus was unique from both Rome and Corinth (Eph. 4:11). Jerusalem had things about it that were unique Jewish things, unlike any of the churches in other cities.

So I've told bits and pieces of the story that focus on my personal struggle to be renewed in the aftermath of failure. If one of these slices of life helps to renew the church, so be it.

Notes

1. Stan Jones, "New Leadership for New Churches," *Faith at Work* (September-October 1988): 13.
2. Harold K. Moulton, *Analytical Greek Lexicon*, rev. ed. (Grand Rapids: Zondervan, 1978), 344.

3. Ibid., 216–17
4. Larry Richards, *Expository Dictionary of Bible Words* (Grand Rapids: Zondervan, 1985), 402.
5. Moulton, *Analytical Greek Lexicon*, 180.
6. Matthew 11:12, KJV.

Chapter 11

Hope for Fallen Trees

> There is hope for a tree: If it is cut down, it will
> sprout again, and its new shoots will not fail.
>
> —*Job 14:7*

SOMEWHERE, AS I grew up in the church, I caught the message that real Christians do not fail—they are always victorious. Imagine my surprise when, pressed to find answers for my proneness to failure, I discovered that the Bible accepts the idea of failure as a part of life. "A righteous man falls seven times, and rises again," observed Solomon (Prov. 24:16).

No one is immune to failure. Human weakness, the old sin nature, and the habits of a lifetime promise that failure will be a familiar companion, even as we walk with God. The ongoing provisions of God's grace are necessary because human weakness trips even the best of us. The Old Testament provided the Levitical sacrifices to cover the expected spiritual lapses of Israel. Under the New Covenant, the possibility of confession and forgiveness (1 John 1:9), the continuous application of the blood of Christ (indicated by the Greek tense in 1 John 1:7), and the advocate role of Christ (1 John 2:1) are provided because Christians have a continuing problem with failure, weakness, and sin.

THE LEAVENED BREAD OF PENTECOST

A most intriguing picture of the way God works with failing people to accomplish his purposes was contained in one aspect of the Feast of Pentecost (also called "the Feast of Weeks," Lev. 23:15–22; Deut. 16:9–12). At other Mosaic festivals (e.g., Passover), only bread without yeast was to be eaten. Yeast (leaven) is an ancient biblical symbol for sin. But at Pentecost, the harvest festival, God's specific instructions were to prepare the festal bread with yeast (Lev. 23:17). To cover the presence of the yeast (sin), lambs were to be sacrificed at the same time the leavened loaves were being offered (Lev. 23:18). Furthermore, the bread was to be brought to the place of worship "from wherever you live" (Lev. 23:17). Merrill Unger suggests that this means they were to be loaves prepared for the daily nourishment of the family, not specially prepared, sacramental bread prepared at the temple and paid for out of the temple treasury.[1]

Celebrants at this festival were specifically to include every segment of the community, including the children, men and women, male and female servants, the Levites, the foreigners, the fatherless and the widows (Deut. 16:11). No one was excluded.

The bread was common, daily bread. It was presented to the Lord by common people who shared a meal together and rejoiced before the Lord. It is a symbolic affirmation of the Lord's acceptance of ordinary, failing people and of his intention to bless them and use them to fulfill his purposes.

None of the heroes of the faith was ever a perfect man or woman. In every case God took unformed, rough, rebellious, straying, or mistaken clay and gradually transformed it into a useful vessel. The stories are there to read: Jacob the deceiver, Moses the escaped murderer, Rahab the harlot, David the adulterer, Isaiah the man of unclean lips, Jeremiah the reluctant child, Peter the coward, Paul the persecuter. Even those whose sins are not so readily apparent (e.g., Joseph, Joshua, Samuel, Ruth, Daniel, Mary) began as incomplete and ordinary humans and had their moments of weakness and wrong-headedness. Samuel, for instance, seemed to live a most consistent and godly life, but he failed with his sons. Mary was a true believer who willingly presented her body to God, but to learn that Jesus was not merely her son but her Lord necessitated a firm and painful rebuke.

The reality pictured in the Feast of Weeks broke into human experience in a special way on the Day of Pentecost. The Lord poured it out on all 120 of his waiting disciples at once. They burst out of the upper room after a flaming encounter with the Holy Spirit—all of them boldly telling the wonders of God in the languages of the gathered feast-goers (Acts 2:4–11). As a result, thousands of ordinary men and women, some of whose failings are well documented, became priests, ministers, and prophets of God. Following them have come thousands more in every generation—incomplete people needing the continual cleansing of the blood of Christ because they have a continuing problem with sin. Through them God is doing his work, even though the process of needed change and renewal is not finished in their lives.

Together, with all their failure-proneness, they are a living offering to God that he joyfully accepts. Out of the ordinariness of their daily lives they bring gifts to share with one another before the Lord. Most are not especially saintly or unusually gifted, and not all their problems are solved. But these people are the leavened bread of Pentecost. In this new "loaf"[2], the church of Jesus Christ, human weakness and divine grace combine to provide God with a table at which to feed the world.

Christ readily chooses to be identified with such leavened bread. He is the Lamb whose blood atones for their sin. He knows them as parts of himself (1 Cor. 6:15; 12:12; Eph. 5:30).

To touch a disciple is to touch the Lord himself (Matt. 10:40; 25:40; Acts 9:4–5). First Corinthians 6:15–20 indicates that they are members of Christ even while they are failing him. Their motivation to live holy lives is the assurance that wherever they are and whatever they are doing he is there; their bodies belong to him, and they are his physical presence in that place.

The completeness of his identification with believing people who fail is not only a deterrent to sin, it is the chosen context for the continuation of Christ's saving work. Imperfect as we are, his people, indwelt by his Spirit, are his hands: the word *diakonia* (servanthood) applies to both his service and ours (Matt. 20:26–27; Rom. 12:7). We are his voice: the word *prophetes* (prophet, speaker for God) applies to both Jesus and his disciples, many if not all of whom are authorized to speak for God (Acts 2:17–18; 3:19–23; 7:37; 1 Cor. 14:24–25, 29–32). We are his heart: the word *agape* (godly love) applies to both his love and ours (John 13:34–35; Rom. 12:9; 1 Cor. 13:1–13).

The way is opened for even weak people to be instruments in the Spirit's hands in the edification of the church and the distribution of the bread of life in the world. A missionary statesman once aptly described the work of evangelism as "one beggar telling another where to find bread."

THE THERAPEUTIC EFFECTS OF FAILURE

For the believer, failure is not fatal. "*When* he fails," admits David (Ps. 37:24), "he shall not be hurled headlong." The Scriptures elsewhere affirm the same truth: failure will come, and when it does there is a floor under the believer—he cannot be destroyed.

> Do not rejoice over me, O my enemy.
> Though I fall I will rise;
> Though I dwell in darkness, the Lord is a light for me.
> I will bear the indignation of the Lord
> Because I have sinned against Him,
> Until He pleads my case and executes justice for me.

He will bring me out to the light,
And I will see His righteousness (Mic. 7:8–9, NASB).

It's not a pretty picture: the man escaping through the flames while his life's labors go up in smoke (1 Cor. 3:15). He is deeply affected by his loss. He doesn't smell like a success anymore. The odor of burnt works clings to him. But the man himself escapes destruction. His work is a disaster! That's not a happy discovery. And yet the grace of God meets him at the point of his failure. That's the good news.

Fortunately, the Lord does not keep secret until "that Day" the true state of our work. He is actively involved all along the way, judging, cleansing, disclosing, and working (even with our failures) to reshape us and our work. Some of us are very obstinate, arrogant, and hard of hearing, and so to our other failures we add the failure to heed his warnings. But he loves us and keeps working.

Several passages tell of the therapeutic effects God is able to create out of the painful and embarrassing experiences of life.

Pressure Produces Sterling
Romans 5:2–5

The Greek word translated "suffering" means pressure, distress of mind, distressing circumstances, trial, and affliction.[3] The restored likeness of God (glory) comes only through a process involving pain and pressure, which produces perseverance, sterling character[4], hope, and the experience of God's love. That's success in God's eyes and is enough to make a man leap for joy![5]

Jesus Emerges
2 Corinthians 4:7–18

The Amplified Bible uses several words for failure here. The treasure of the Spirit is possessed by us in "frail, human vessels of earth." Our Christian experience includes being "hedged in [pressed] on every side—troubled and oppressed in every way"; "we suffer embarrassments . . . perplexed . . . unable to find a way out"; "we are [persecuted and hard driven] pursued . . . struck down to the ground." Through it all God sees to it that we are never "crushed . . . driven to despair . . . deserted to stand alone . . . destroyed." Reverses, inadequacies, and failure are among the stuff of the Christian life.

God is able to distill at least four positive results from all this battle gore: (1) Jesus is seen living in us (vv. 10–11); (2) spiritual blessing and favor touch the lives of more people through us, and they in turn share his grace with others, thus multiplying the worship of God (v. 15); (3) even though outwardly we experience failure, our inner self is being thoroughly renovated (v. 16); and (4) we are learning to look at everything in this life from an eternal perspective (vv. 17–18), which is God's way of looking at it.

God's Power Is Visible in Weak People
2 Corinthians 12:7–10

In spite of many wonderful spiritual experiences and special revelations from God, Paul could not get deliverance from a troublesome and diabolical personal weakness he called his "thorn." It undermined his self-confidence and kept him from being the strong leader people expected him to be. Three times he prayed about it. Three times his prayer failed to move God. But as he collected his failed prayers and nursed his stinging disappointment, he heard God say, "My grace is enough for you. My strength is demonstrated as effective through your weakness."

It was not what the apostle wanted to hear. But it raised his perspective on failure to new heights. If God could show off his strength through that weakness, then, instead of feeling embarrassed about it, he decided to make it the focal point of his rejoicing and hope. With this new perspective, he could stop trying to muscle his way to success in ministry. All he had to do was be open and dependent . . . and watch God work.

A Harvest of Righteousness and Peace
Hebrews 12:4–13

As children the Father genuinely loves, we may expect to be disciplined to assure healthy spiritual development. Hebrews 11 is a catalog of saints who experienced the discipline of the Lord. Not one person on the list reached his major goal prior to death (11:39–40). Each one represents not only the blessing of God, but the pain of shortfall. The major accomplishment of their lives was to be faithful to God in the face of rejection and martyrdom. We are told to be willing to resist in the struggle against sin, even to the point of shedding blood (12:4). We are promised that the effect of difficult circumstances will be (1) a share in God's holiness (12:10); (2) a harvest of righteousness and peace (12:11); (3) spiritual training (12:11); and (4) with the help of one another, healing and strengthening at the point of our spiritual disability (12:13).

Trouble Showcases Faith
1 Peter 1:6–9

Peter's insistence is that grief and trouble—"all kinds"—showcase the priceless genuineness of personal faith. We cannot know if our faith is real unless it goes through the refining fires of suffering. When we discover that our faith is authentic, when we see Jesus revealing himself to us and we experience deepened certainty of our salvation, we enhance our ability to worship with "inexpressible joy" that would not have been possible without the pain.

Difficulties and Destiny

Romans 8:28–29 summarizes this biblical teaching:

And we know that in all things God works for the good of those who love him, who have been called according to his purpose. For those God foreknew he also predestined to be conformed to the likeness of his Son.

No matter what happens to us, what flaws cling to our personalities, what we try and fail to accomplish, what opposition we face, what mistakes we make, what weaknesses plague us, what pressure, distress, or pain we suffer—all of it has a sign over it that reads

GOD AT WORK!

FROM BRAGGING TO BROKENNESS

Peter's experience illustrates how God changes a man through failure. If ever a man was apparently loyal to Jesus, it was he. At the Last Supper he boasted, "I will lay down my life for you!" (John 13:37). Jesus' response shocked him. "Before the rooster crows, you will disown me three times!" He did (Luke 22:54–62). He miserably failed. After the resurrection, Jesus met him on the shore of Galilee and asked three times, "Do you love me?" (John 21:15–19). The first two times he used the word *agape*, a word for perfect love.

Peter's swagger was gone. No more boasting. No more promises. In all honesty the fisherman replied, "You know that I love [*phileo*] you." He responded with a word that means friendship. It's as if Peter were saying, "I would like to be able to boast that my love for you is perfect. But these last few days have shown me the truth about myself. The best I can do is tell you that I love you as a very dear friend."

Jesus asked the question again, meeting Peter's new honesty with grace: "Do you love me [as your friend]?" Deeply wounded, but unwilling to fail in the same way again, Peter responded, "You know that I love you [as a friend]."

If true success is bound up with a humble attitude of dependence on God, then failure is tied to a spiritual arrogance that fails to admit how needy we really are. Peter's life didn't end with the crushing failure that let the hot air out of his pride. It *began* after that, with his new sense of vulnerability and weakness. Jesus immediately gave him a new work to do:

"Feed my sheep." We know what happened then. It's in the book of Acts.

Peter could never have been the useful instrument he became had he not gone through the belittling, humiliating experience of collapse at the very point at which he felt strong.

The same may someday be observed of you and me, if we learn to bring ourselves before the Lord in a new attitude of weakness and humility.

In a sermon called "Growthing Through Failures," Jack Dunnigan listed five important things failure accomplishes for us, based on Peter's experience:

1. Failure makes us accurately assess ourselves and our situation.
2. Failure helps us to see our dangerous weaknesses.
3. Failure short-circuits our tendency toward self-right-eousness.
4. Failure provokes us to find answers.
5. Failure teaches us to love without conditions.[6]

When Tom Watson was president of IBM, a young vice president was put in charge of a project involving ten million dollars. Under the young executive the project failed. He lost it all, and he fully expected to be fired. While waiting to be summoned into the president's office, he packed up the personal things in his desk and said goodbye to his associates.

The call came. Before the president could speak, the young executive said, "I suppose you want my resignation."

Tom Watson replied, "Your resignation? We have just spent ten million dollars giving you an education. We are not about to let you go now!"[7]

The faithfulness of God to transform trouble into spiritual growth for the responsive Christian leads us to believe in this equation:

Failure = Education

Notes

1. Merrill Unger, *Unger's Bible Dictionary* (Chicago: Moody Press, 1957), 357.
2. 1 Corinthians 10:17.
3. Harold K. Moulton, *Analytical Greek Lexicon*, rev. ed. (Grand Rapids: Zondervan, 1978), 195
4. William Barclay, *The Letter to the Romans* (Philadelphia: Westminster, 1975), 74.
5. To "exult" (Rom. 5:2) means literally "to leap for joy."
6. Jack Dunnigan, "Honest to God" (tape). Leadership Enrichment Ministries, P.O. Box 745, Rimrock, AZ 86335.
7. Ibid.

Chapter 12

Walking With a Limp

So Jacob called the place Peniel, saying, "It is because I saw God face to face, and yet my life was spared."

The sun rose above him as he passed Peniel, and he was limping because of his hip.

—Genesis 32:30–31

UNTIL I BEGAN to understand that God accepts me even with my weaknesses, including my dismal record of past failure, I felt hopeless and lost—a disappointment to myself, my church, my family, and my God. The guilty self-flagellation in which I have been engaged most of my life is a nasty habit, hard to break.

But now there is hope. I haven't yet broken through to Paul's *delight* in weaknesses (2 Cor. 12:10), but I have begun to accept myself with them, and to organize my life more realistically in the light of what I now know about myself.

It has been seven years since I spent those forty memory-

173

jarring hours in primal integration therapy[1], walked out into the light, and started trying to live with new insights. I cannot give an enthusiastic report of clear-cut healing in every area where it is needed. What I can report is that I now understand where I am most vulnerable to spiritual failure.

I have already reported how my response to the demands of the pastorate created pressures that took me beyond the limits of emotional well-being and into trouble. As long as I failed to recognize, admit, and accept my weaknesses and limitations, I was always in over my head, filled with fear and anger, and spending time and energy working where I did not really belong. I had all the classic symptoms of "pastoral burnout." It was humiliating and frustrating to have to admit that what others seemed able to do, I could not. So I quit.

God met my resignation with grace. I was sure he would reject me if I left the ministry. Instead, he kept leading me to biblical and personal assurances that he loved me with all my inadequacies, forgave all my failures, and intended to use my newly acknowledged weaknesses as points at which to demonstrate his adequacy and strength.

POWER, PERFECTION, AND WEAKNESS

I am irresistibly attracted to the bizarre proposition Paul puts forth in 2 Corinthians 12:9: "Power is made perfect in weakness."

It sounds like nonsense. Yet Paul insists *God personally* spoke these words to him. Further, he dares to rest the whole case for the validity of his apostleship on such apparent folly!

Some church people in Corinth refused to accept him as a bona fide apostle because he was so uncharismatic. When they looked at Paul they saw, not the "together" leader they felt the church needed, but a weak man who refused to look, speak, or act like a superstar.

His response to their criticism is startling: "It is my weaknesses—so obvious and irritating to you all—which actually give God a chance to use his power!"

It's an idea that shatters many cherished illusions. It declares that God is not interested in producing self-contained spiritual giants who appear powerful and are recognized by the world as such. He's looking for people through whom he can demonstrate his strength in ways that convince observers that the power is God's. The weakness of the weak provides exactly the setting he desires for revealing his adequacy.

The original word for power in 2 Corinthians 12:9 is *dunamis*. English derivatives include "dynamite," "dynamo," and "dynamic." Employing several of the lexical concepts contained in *dunamis*, we can state the 2 Corinthians 9:12 perspective like this:

> Power, strength, ability, energy, effectiveness, might, authority, and majesty are perfected in weakness.[2]

The word for "perfect" is *teleos*. It means finished, completed, concluded, fulfilled, carried out into full operation, realized.[3] Weakness, says 2 Corinthians 12:9, is the catalyst or environment that allows God's power to reach its zenith of effectiveness.

In Paul's principle, weakness is *astheneia*. The word carries most of the ideas attached to the concept weakness—i.e., want of strength, feebleness, bodily infirmity, a state of ill health, sickness, frailty, imperfections, suffering, affliction, distress, and calamity.[4] Each is something which can be used in believers to make the power of God effective and fulfilled.

Amazing and liberating!

God lacks nothing, needs no one, and is in himself absolute, self-existent, and fully sovereign over everything in the created universe. His power is perfect and completely able to accomplish whatever he decides. He has more energy than the deepest human need can exhaust or the wildest imagination can fathom (Eph. 3:20). But his secret, whispered to Paul, is that there is a sense (established by his own grand design) in which his power is imperfect, incomplete, and unable to operate at full effectiveness except in the presence of human weakness. That is, the infiniteness and limitlessness of God's strength remains untapped, unknown, and unexperienced until a situation is provided in which there are acknowledged needs the divine *dunamis* may serve. In the lives of people who trust him, every imaginable human frailty or failing provides God's power with a venue for demonstration.

GALLERY OF POWERLESSNESS

To avoid misunderstanding, Paul tells about some of his own weaknesses. It's one of the strangest descriptions of a "spiritual giant" ever recorded:

He is not a skillful speaker (2 Cor. 11:6). This either means he is not an eloquent orator or that he had a speech impediment.

He has a tendency to be in bondage to those who are paying his support. He refuses to receive financial support from the Corinthians for his ministry (11:7–9). He says he does this to "elevate" those to whom he is ministering (v. 7) and to keep from "being a burden" (v. 9). He was concerned for them, not for the living he could make from them.

He is a "weak leader" (2 Cor. 11:21)—at least in the opinion of some Corinthian Christians. There are church people who think a good leader is one who "carries himself" like a leader, speaks like a leader, makes demands on people, and uses them to further his own ministry. By these standards Paul's leadership is weak. He doesn't pull rank, throw his weight around, or take away anyone's freedom in the course of leading. Those who measure by the world's standard misunderstand that kind of servant-leadership and call it "weakness."

Beginning in 11:23, Paul's list of frailties, infirmities and failures grows quickly. He works like a slave. He has a prison record. He makes people so angry that he has been beaten repeatedly. Stoned publicly. Shipwrecked three times. Never home. In almost constant danger from the elements, highwaymen, and his own countrymen who consider him a traitor. Hated. Even church people hate him and work against him. Hardship. Sleepless nights. Hunger and fasting. Thirst. Cold.

His external struggle is matched by continuing internal

conflict and weakness. He feels the pressure of concern for all the churches (vv. 28–29). Whenever anyone suffers or is weak or fails spiritually, "I burn for them!" A strong leader could keep his sense of responsibility in better balance, but Paul dies with every saint who stumbles.

The apostle spills forth still more: "In Damascus, the response to my ministry was that the king considered me a public enemy and decided to arrest me. I barely escaped" (11:32–33). In 2 Corinthians 12 he adds to his infamous list:

Unanswered prayer (vv. 8–9)

Insults (v. 10)

Distresses (v. 10)

Persecutions (v. 10)

Difficulties (v. 10)

Fear of disappointment (v. 20)

Fear of rejection (v. 20)

Fear of facing difficult situations (v. 20)

Fear that God will humiliate him publicly by allowing him to show weakness in front of the very people who are looking for weaknesses as an excuse for rejecting him (v. 21)

Fear that he will break down and cry publicly (v. 21)

Fear that they will not listen to him, but will persist in their rebellious ways (v. 21)

How many of these thing are usable for displaying the power of God? The apostle insists they *all* are!

O Lord! Could my horrendous list of failures possibly be included?

THE THORN

Conditioned as we are to the way church leaders normally function, it is surprising to hear "the great apostle of the church" express himself with the kind of candor with which he tells about his "thorn."

Because my early experiences with Christ were so out-of-this-world and because I have a tendency to become conceited about them, God has given me an unwanted gift to keep my pride in check. He has given me a "thorn in my flesh." It is the kind of thing that is so tormenting it could only be the work of the devil. God permits the enemy to afflict me to keep me from exalting myself (2 Cor. 12:1–7, paraphrased).

Paul purposely does not specify the exact nature of his diabolical infirmity so that each of us would be left free to think it might have been the same as our own and could apply his message immediately to ourselves. Some of the things Paul writes about himself in his letters suggest several possibilities, i.e., bad eyes or a speech impediment or epilepsy or a bad marriage. It is possible that it was some emotional weakness like supersensitivity that disrupted his relationships.

Whatever it is, he hates it. He prays to be set free from its embarrassing presence. The heavenly Father's persistent answer is No.

My grace is sufficient for you, for my power is made perfect in weakness.

The revelation of the thorn is: When we are strong in our own eyes, God must, in his loving-kindness, bring us to weakness so that we can discover his strength.

AT PEACE WITH WHAT I AM

When we grasp the truth that our inadequacies are the launching pad for the power of God, our whole attitude toward ourselves has opportunity to change . . .

I am *well content* with weakness (12:10, NASB, italics added).

When I let my weaknesses be known and give up my desperate fight to appear strong, it is a great relief. I begin to relax with being who I am. I can even find joy in my weaknesses.

At least that is Paul's experience. He advances beyond

mere acknowledgment of inadequacies to delight (NIV), enjoyment (PHILLIPS), pleasure (AMPLIFIED), and contentment (NASB) in frailties and struggles.

He is at peace with his weaknesses because (1) he does not see them as enemies, but has broken through to the insight that they are in his life "for Christ's sake" (v. 10), and (2) he grasps by faith the revelation that "when I am weak, then I am strong" (v. 10).

CHANGE TO A RELAXED LIFESTYLE

Now we live in a tiny village in the central mountains of Arizona, ninety miles from the roar of big-city traffic. There's not a stoplight for thirty miles. It's often so quiet you can hear the quail scratching the sand for their breakfast. The pace of life, while busy and full, is infinitely more relaxed than in the metropolis whose distant lights create a pale yellow glow on our night horizon.

Sometimes I feel guilty for fleeing the city for this easier country place. Occasionally I miss "the big-city challenge" with its throbbing cultural scene and the feeling of being where the action is. Awareness of urban spiritual need at times becomes intense. I pray for those who minister there. And I ask God, "Should I return?"

If God sends me, I will go back to the city and do whatever he wants me to do. Meanwhile, Audrey and I have found God's people here, and all around us are people as needy as any in the city. It's a lifestyle that more nearly fits my strengths, weaknesses, gifts, and spiritual condition. It is okay for me to be pastor of a small church in a small place. And it's okay for me to be at peace. I am exactly where I belong. I am only good for helping people if I am honestly what I am—weaknesses and all. I can only survive if, in the midst of my work, I can remain at rest.

If Paul is right, these limitations are the very points that give God opportunity to demonstrate the effectiveness of his power.

LEADERS WITH LIMPS

If reconciliation between what a minister is and what is expected of him or her is ever to become reality, the church will have to come to accept weakness and limitation in its leaders. Pastoral burnout is something the church generates by its unrealistic, superhuman expectations and demands. The job description of many pastors amounts to a formula for breakdown!

The limp the man or woman of God has been given may well be God's way of making him or her a better servant-leader. In the first place, specific limitation of the body's members is God's scheme for making them one, by creating them incomplete without one another. All the "spiritual gift" passages—especially 1 Corinthians 12—are clear on this. Acknowledged weakness, far from being detrimental, leaves room for others to operate with their gifts and strengths. This is why Paul insists,

> Those parts of the body which seem to be weaker are indispensable. (1 Cor. 12:22).

Reading that, I have often pictured someone visibly weaker—the immature or divisive person, the retiring wallflower who sometimes suffers from neglect because he is not the "squeaking wheel," or the less gifted person who doesn't seem to have much to add to the advancement of the work. I wonder, however, if many of us in church leadership are not included among the weaker parts. How many of us entered the ministry or sought church leadership precisely because of our insecurity, our neurotic need to be noticed and loved, our legalistic fear of rejection by God, our guilty drive to prove our worth, or our fear of not being heard? At times I have felt that I was indeed the weakest person in the church!

I am convinced that burnout comes because one member, riddled with weaknesses, is trying to do too many things that others have been placed in the body to do, but have either refused or not been permitted to do. Don't blame the leader alone. Blame an ecclesiastical mentality which demands material and numerical success rather than simple obedience to God—and which, in fact, does not know the difference between the two. Blame a clerical tradition that robs the body of its functions and tries to dump them all on one member. Blame the blindness of the many to their God-appointed spiritual opportunities and responsibilities. Blame an institutionalized Christianity, straining to be accepted by the world, that is trying to do too many things that were never intended by the Head and that are not necessary to an effective, Christ-responsive church.

THE WEAKENING OF THE SAINTS

Hudson Taylor said, "All God's giants have been weak people."

The Bible indicates that "the weakening of the saints" is often something God must do in order to make them responsive and useful. Note the process through which he has taken so many of the heroes of the faith.

Abraham and Sarah. God promised them an heir. Then he let them wait for so long that Abraham was a hundred years old and "as good as dead" and "Sarah's womb was also dead" (Rom. 4:19). God gave them time to make some very humbling, painful mistakes, such as the affair with Hagar and Ishmael (Gen. 16), so they could come to a complete awareness of their own weakness and helpless dependence on God.

Jacob. God promised him a place of supremacy in the family. Taking things into his own hands, Jacob connived and manipulated to get it by craftiness. His acquisition was meaningless as he fled to escape the rightful wrath of his brother, Esau. Little by little, God brought the willful conniver to a sense of his dependence on God, culminating the night Jacob wrestled with the Lord's angel and came away crippled and weakened, but changed—his swagger replaced by a limp, his conniving spirit replaced by trembling humility and dependence on God (Gen. 25:27–32).

Moses. Reared as Egyptian royalty, the adopted son of

Pharaoh's daughter, Moses saw his blood relatives, the Jews, mistreated and enslaved. Being a man of intelligence, eloquence, and regal authority, he decided he would be their deliverer. Early in the process he murdered an Egyptian, the Jews refused to accept him as their savior, and he fled for his life to Midian (Ex. 2:10–15). Forty years later, as an escaped murderer, his eloquence lost, his authority reduced to sheepherding, bereft of the recognizable traits of leadership, he was called by God to return to Egypt to deliver Israel. His reluctance showed that trust in his own strength was gone. Deliverance would have to be an act of God. Moses knew he could not do it. To God, this was a sign Moses was ready for service (Ex. 4).

The apostles. The Holy Spirit did not fill and energize the Lord's closest followers and use them to turn the world upside down until they got past their bragging intentions and their worldly viewpoint and understood how prone they were to forsake him. Shameful failure, shocking moral and spiritual weakness, and the experience of watching their Messiah die created a vacuum devoid of human wisdom, bravado, and adequacy into which the living Jesus could move. Acknowledged weakness leading to total dependence on God was the continuing milieu of the dynamic New Testament church (Acts 4:23–31).

Trace the stories of all the people God has won and used. Every one of them has gone through some type of weakening process to break the outer shell of arrogance, self-righteousness, and dependence on personal strength, charisma, and talent. God uses failure, sickness, breakdown, sin, personal tragedy, and sorrow to reduce his people to usefulness. Unless the servant of God learns to depend utterly on God and to forsake self-dependence of any kind, he or she remains too strong to be of much value.

Instead of complaining about the leader's limp and criticizing his weak points, the church members should be accepting, affirming, and thanking God for the gift of human limitation, then asking him how they ought to be functioning in order to fill the divinely designed gaps. If the man of God is supposed to see his own weaknesses as reason to rejoice—as Paul says—then the church should come to see them that way too. The church will be fighting against the plan of God until it does so.

To those who believe that God can use only the strong and the perfect, this may seem like the height of foolishness, but the truth is that weakness and failure do not disqualify a person for service. On the contrary: "Power is perfected in weakness." Even the power of an apostle (2 Cor. 12:11–12).

> God does not work through those who think they are the pillars of the church. He works through weakness. When weakness, personal insufficiency and utter inability are consciously felt, realized and known, then the power of God and his purpose for the thorn have been fulfilled.
>
> —*Alan Redpath*[5]

FAILURES AS REMINDERS OF GRACE

I am learning to see my failures as markers along the way to remind me of the grace of God. For years they ate at my insides like ulcers. Whenever I thought of them, I bled. An acrid, bitter taste clung to my tongue when I spoke of them. My knees grew rubbery as I relived each embarrassment and grief. But the Word and Spirit are changing my perspective. I am learning to return to those memories of struggle and pain as to the grave of a loved one whose influence has been vital to the full experience of life. I'm getting so I can actually stand near the point of fallen dreams and worship, giving thanks to God for the way his mercy has refined and transmuted the raw material of pain into the sterling of a richer life with him.

My failures have not destroyed me. They have re-created me. They have introduced me to myself. They have forced me to move toward forever dependence on the Lord.

Notes

1. Primal Integration Therapy: To find out more about it, contact Cecil Osborne, Yokefellows, Inc., 245 El Camino Real, Milbrae,

CA 94030, or see his books *The Art of Learning to Love Yourself* (Grand Rapids: Zondervan, 1976) and *Release From Fear and Anxiety* (Waco, Tex.: Word, 1976).

2. Harold K. Moulton, *The Analytical Greek Lexicon,* rev. ed. (Grand Rapids: Zondervan, 1978), 107–8.

3. Ibid., 400–401.

4. Ibid., 55.

5. Alan Redpath, *Blessings Out of Buffetings: Studies in Second Corinthians* (Old Tappan, N.J.: Revell, 1965).